T0328493

Iswaydaarsi

2

Muuse Ismaaciil Galaal with members of the Somali Language
Commission and with B. W. Andrzejewski

ESSAYS IN HONOUR OF

Muuse Ismaaciil Galaal

Edited by
Jama Musse Jama

Preface
I M Lewis

2011

PONTE INVISIBILE
REDSEA-ONLINE.COM

REDSEA-ONLINE.COM Culture Foundation
Fidiyaha Aqoonta iyo Ereyga Dhigan - Xarunta dhexe
Daarta Oriental Hotel - Hargeysa, Somaliland
telephone: 00 252 2 525109 | 00 252 2 4099088
email: bookshop@redsea-online.com

Ponte Invisibile
Inquiries to the editor
Jama Musse Jama
Via Pietro Giordani 4, 56123 Pisa, Italy
www.ponteinvisibile.com
email: editor@redsea-online.com | editor@ponteinvisibile.com

Published by Ponte Invisibile (redsea-online), 2011, Pisa
II

Copyright © 2011 Ponte Invisibile Edizioni
A REDSEA-ONLINE Publishing Group Company.
ISBN 88-88934-27-8 | EAN 9788888934273

WWW.REDSEA-ONLINE.COM | WWW.KAYD.ORG
PRINTED AND BOUND IN ITALY.

Suggested classification for the librarians
Essays in honour of Muuse Ismaaciil Galaal / Jama Musse Jama (edited by)
pp. 160 cm. 140x210
Includes Index and bilingual English-Somali poems.

ISBN 88-88934-27-8 EAN 9788888934273
I. Essays in honour of Muuse Ismaaciil Galaal II. Jama Musse Jama (edited by). Preface by I. M. Lewis; Contributions by Martin Orwin, Sheila Andrzejewski, Anita Suleiman, Georgi Kapchits, Alexander Zholkovsky, Sarah Maguire / III. Literature / Poetry.

Qaybta Af Soomaaliga ah waxa lagu saxay Ubbo – Quraar iyo Higgaadshe saxa Af Soomaaliga. Ka eeg www.redsea-online.com/ubbo

In memory of Muuse Xaaji Ismaaciil Galaal

INDEX

PREFACE

Ioan M. Lewis

It is a great pleasure and honour for me to write a few words in memory of the late Muuse Gaalal, who was such a remarkable literary figure in the history of Somali culture and oral poetry. I first met him in the early 1950s when he was working as B. W. Andrzejewski's indispensible research assistant. Frequently, he might more accurately have been described as his teacher. Goosh introduced me to him and we got on well, although at the time, I could only speak to him in English which, of course he spoke well, his words reflecting his great knowledge and enthusiasm for Somali culture, history and poetry in which he was himself an important figure. Andrzejewski and he had a very close friendship and had developed a number of similar personal characteristics. Their mutual respect and friendship was strengthened by the fact that they were both poets. Muuse also possessed a deep knowledge of Somali society and culture. He was indeed a self-taught anthropologist with an endless curiosity.

His lively charismatic personality and impressive sense of style, made him a most effective ambassador for Somali culture and ideas and for the society of which he had such a profound knowledge. His personality, which included a lively sense of humour, made him an ideal vehicle for promoting Somali ideas. He was however completely without pomposity and, unlike some of his younger countrymen never claimed to be a 'Somali Intellectual'.

Once when he was ill in London I remember setting off to what was then St George's Hospital to pay him a visit. When we got there, however, we could not find him. The nursing staff said they did not know where he had got to. As they put it, 'that naughty Mr Muuse had disappeared again'. Cooped up as he was by his confinement in hospital, he must have been tempted to escape into the park outside. He was a tall man and a great walker, as befitted his nomadic background. My wife recalls the impressive figure he cut striding through the winter snow in Scotland where we lived at the time (1961) and Muuse visited us. We took him to see Loch Lomond, which in that excessively cold winter was frozen over— as the photograph with our daughter, Joanna ('Dalmara') born in Hargeisa, shows.

Muuse had the character and bearing of a distinguished Somali elder and a wonderful stock of stories and anecdotes as well as profound knowledge on a wide range of subjects. When he died on his last journey en route to Saudi Arabia to receive urgent medical treatment, his plane turned back to Mogadishu. The whole of Mogadishu was in a state of turmoil such as no other national figure's death had ever provoked.

I.M. Lewis, Fellow of the British Academy.

INTRODUCTION

Jama Musse Jama

This publication is the second of a new series of books called *"Iswaydaarsi"* (Exchange), published by Ponte Invisibile (redsea-online). This series intends to provide specific knowledge of international classical literature to the Somali speaking readership, and at the same time translate Somali literature and wisdom into other languages.

Literature and traditional knowledge that a group of people possess, when translated into other languages, enriches the wisdom and important traditions of that group of people. In addition, translation contributes to the growth and development of the standard of world poetry. Muuse Ismaaciil Galaal, strived to preserve Somali poetry and the traditional knowledge and customs of the Somali people, and at the same time he translated it into other languages which not only enriched and benefited the Somali wisdom but also enhanced the global knowledge of humans and poetry on a global stage. This year (2011) is the 30th anniversary of Muuse Galaal's death.

Somali Week Festival, which is an integral part of the Black History Month celebrations, takes place in London in October every year. The festival is organized by Kayd Somali Arts and Culture and Redsea-online Cultural Foundation, and the theme the festival wants to introduce this year is 'Translation'. Translated works enable individuals to learn about a particular culture and its people. There is currently a severe shortage of Somali work translated into foreign languages and even fewer examples of world literature translated into Somali. It is this lack of cultural exchange that the festival wishes to address by choosing translation as the theme of the year.

Recognizing therefore the work by Muuse Galaal in this context, Somali Week Festival, as part of the commemoration of this anniversary, invited academicians, researchers and people who worked with Muuse Galaal or know his work, to write about his life and work. This volume contains contributions by Martin Orwin, Alexander Zholkovsky, Georgi Kapchits, Sheila Andrzejewski, Anita S Adam, Sarah Maguire and my self with the preface of Professor Ioan M. Lewis. It also contains a very less known work by Muuse Galaal and published in 1954: the article *Arabic script for Somali* appeared in Islamic Quarterly, vol. 1.

The book contains also translations from the Somali Week Festival 2011 guest-artists in honour of the role Muuse Galaal played in research, preservation of indigenous knowledge, history and Somali culture and heritage. These works, translated by Sarah Maguire and Mohamed Hassan "Alto" and other English poets, are part of the collaborative work between Somali Week Festival and Poetry Translation Centre (London).

I am deeply thankful to Ayan Mahamoud Mahamed, Managing Direcotor of Kayd Somali Arts and Culture for her tireless effort in organazing this festival. I am also thankful to Poetry Translation Center for their permission to publisher the translation of the poems.

MUUSE ISMAACIIL GALAAL
(CAYN, q.1920 – JIDDAH, 1980)

Jama Musse Jama

Giddigeed adduunyada intii geesi lagu faanay,
Gocasho iyo magac baa ka hadha gobi u aydaa e,
Waad gudatay Muusow xilkii kula gudboonaaye,
Guushii ifkiyo aakhirba lagu guddoonsiiye.
[…]
Mar haddaanad geerida horteed, geesiga aqoonsan,
Goblan weeye Soomaaliyeey garashadaadiiye!

Cali Sugulle "Duncarbeed"

1. Introduction

Muuse Ismaaciil Galaal was a researcher, scientist, historian, writer and poet whose most important lasting legacy is the role he played in the creation of the modern written Somali alphabet and written Somali text and in preserving numerous accounts of Somali cultural and heritage, which would otherwise have been lost forever. Later in life he was a respected elder who was regularly consulted for advice and decisions.

Muuse Galaal offered particularly important insights regarding the collection of indigenous knowledge and the depth of Somali wisdom [8] which he introduces in the text below:

> *In trying to set down what I have learned of Somali weather*
> *lore I have become aware of many difficulties, and the*
> *complexity and uniqueness of the subject is one of them.*
> *But more than this, the fact that the beliefs and practices*
> *are unwritten, and handed down from generation to*
> *generation by scattered groups of nomads, and differ*
> *somewhat between groups in terms of their oral exposition,*
> *makes it extremely difficult to offer a comprehensive and*

consistent statement of what is generally held. It is moreover no easy task to explain this unwritten 'Bush Science' in a manner acceptable both to the culture that one writes about and to the modern reader with quite different cultural ideas and a quite different scientific outlook.

Muuse Galaal says that the biggest difficulty he was confronted with in his life was when trying to present the unwritten science of nomadic lifestyle, in a written, structured text as form of learning to modern readers. The biggest challenge laid in trying to shift the tradition and culture of the nomadic lifestyle from the art of oral narrations to written text and thought. At the time of his writing, the written Somali word was still in its infancy, and there was no consensus on how Somali should be written.

The Somali language, complete with its culture and traditions is built upon the people who speak it, and it is passed on from one generation to the next orally, in phrases or sayings or in creative story telling which people narrated and handed down to the new generation. There was no written text which preserved the poetry and the traditional cultural knowledge of the Somali people, and there was no generally accepted written alphabet of Somali until recently. This resulted in loss of customs, traditions and the cultural knowledge of the Somalis, such as star signs, weather forecasting and traditional herbal medicine for animals and humans which were never recorded and have since been entirely lost.

Muuse Galaal warned early on in his life about the loss of traditional Somali knowledge, reasoning that if it is not researched competently and preserved for the future it will surely disappear altogether. In truth the written documentation and records that were found in Muuse Galaal's safe have become vital records which have preserved and saved certain aspects of Somali heritage and knowledge.

The process of written accounts and records of research and work that Muuse Galaal was involved in is best remembered and characterised by the collaborative work he carried out with B. W. Andrzejewski which has become the focal starting point for any research on the Somali language, custom, tradition, cultural knowledge and poetry [7].

Muuse Galaal will also be remembered for the numerous tapes that he recorded during his time at radio stations in Hargeysa and Mogadishu and the research findings which he did not have a chance to publish but were fortunately discovered in his safe.

Therefore, it is essential to shine a light on some of these written records and work that Muuse Galaal collated about Somali culture, customs and heritage. His efforts towards the creation and the standardisation of written formal Somali have been written about elsewhere. We focus here on the the great wealth of research and texts he leaves which are less well-known.

2. Who was Muuse Ismaaciil Galaal?

Muuse Galaal (Muuse Xaaji Ismaaciil Galaal) was born around 1920 in Cayn, in Somaliland, and died in 1980, at the airport of Jidda, in the Kingdom of Saudi Arabia, en route to Italy for medical treatment [6]. He wrote substantial works on Somali traditional culture richly illustrated with excerpts from oral poetry. His name appears in different variations in his published work including the following: Muuse Haaji Ismaaᶜiil Galaal, Musa H. I. Galaal, Muusa Galaal and Muusa H. I. Galaal.

3. Works and collection of poetry

Muuse Galaal's works have made three distinct contributions to the preservation of Somali culture. First, Muuse Galaal's books "Hikmad Soomaali" [10], "Qaalle Adduun" [11] and his unpublished notes "Seeska hiddaha Soomaalida" [15] are now key milestones in our understanding of Somali wisdom and thought, their valuable insights confirmed by later research by other scholars. The second valuable contribution of Muuse Galaal is during his years as presenter at Radio Hargeisa and Radio Muqdishu, when he collected tape recordings of Somali poetry and folk tales. The third major contribution of Muuse Galaal is his research on indigenous knowledge in the fields of astronomy, astrology, weather forecasting, animal husbandry as well as the documentation of magic, traditional medicine and herbal medicine for animals etc. [9] In the following sections we shall consider each of these different areas Muuse Galaal influenced in his research and in his efforts to preserve the traditional knowledge of Somalis.

3.1. Researcher

The research works that Muuse Galaal undertook included the documentation of 28 lunar stations in which a new-moon is seen [8], which structure the traditional calendar which revolves around the night of *dabshid* (or fire-lighting festival) [9]. His research also included the Somali names of the months, planets, seasons, certain clearly visible stars, different types of wind *(Foore, Jiilaashin, Laydh, Walwal, Ufo, Leexo,* etc), different degrees of heat *(Hanfi, Hanas* and *Kul)*, different degrees of cold weather *(Qabow, Geydh, Dheel* and *Haamadday)*, different types of rainfall *(Shuux, Tumay, Hogol, Mahiigaan, Jir,* etc.), laws and types of traditional law making, as well as trees and Somali traditional herbal medicine [15].

3.1.1 **Astrology and whether forecasting**

Muuse Galaal took part in researching and assembling traditional Somali astrology, in which nomads would attach significance to certain stars. He presented the findings of his research in a modern academic form, explaining the foundation of the thought and traditions of the Somali nomads. He extensively explored the 28 lunar stations which is a fundamental concept in Somali astrology and weather prediction, and studied by the nomadic experts with great care and thoroughness. The idea consists of

> "twenty eight different groups of stars or stations
> fixed along the ecliptic path of the moon, and served
> to mark the life span of the Somali lunar month,
> number of days in each year, seasons and for weather
> predications and astrological forecasts. Each station

has from one to over ten stars in its makeup. In addition, however, to the 28 stations along the visible path of the moon during each lunar month, there are said by Somalis to be one or two nights in every month during which the moon is not visible. These are the 'empty stations' when the moon is not in conjunction with any star or group of stars visible to the Somali observer. The period is known in Somali as "Dibbad or Dubbad" and means "an invisible moon", thus the Somali lunar calendar month varies from 29 to 30 days" [9].

Muuse Galaal wrote two unpublished books about astronomy, astrology and weather forecasting based on the traditional Somali local knowledge ([8], [9]), both of these books deserve support and recognition as well as cross-checking their content while the transcripts are still intact.

The research methods that Muuse Galaal used were extremely thorough tracing the tradition of poetry and basing his analysis and research on all subjects on traditional poetry. He used to find a stanza of poetry which has been spoken previously, or phrases and sayings which support his research findings and conclusions. An example of this is when Muuse Galaal was discussing traditional Somali weather forecasting which was based on the nomads gazing at the stars before sunrise, which will tell them whether it would be a drought season, a dry season, or a plentiful season. He used the following stanza as evidence [15]:

Xiddig habarti waa Waabariis, waxay ku bilataaba
Ama waysha qalo bay ku odhan, waytabaaq dhigaye
Ama weelka culo bay ku odhan, iyo wac iyo aabi

Or the following wise saying [15]:

Subbuux Jimce laba kawaydaa, wankaa qalad leh!

Or the following traditional camel song [9]:

Xaydho-dayihii, Kuu xiddigin jirey,
Xareed baridiyo, Xays inoo sheeg.

Translation:

(My beautiful camels)
The reader of the Xaydho[1]
Who is also the expert on stars,
Announces a long-lasting supply of rainwater,
An unexpected season of heavy rain

Or the following traditional cattle song [9]:

Haddaan ururkiyo, Afaggaal ridey,
Mugga eeddaa, Ilaah bayska leh',
Anna orodkay, Waa intii hore.

Translation:

My lovely cow,
Now you can see that the Pleiades (Urur) and the twin stars of Virgo
have set,
And still there is no sign of the spring rains. I have laboured hard
To keep you well,
So that you may live through the harsh dry season,
Be witness, then, it is the Will of God,

3.1.2 Magic

Muse Ismail Galaal in his research presented [15] the results of his findings concerning magic. He talked concisely about his findings in his unpublished notes "Minanka faalka" in which he discussed 17 different variations of magic. The importance of this research lies in the identification of relevant Somali names and word creation, some of these names includes: *jamiic, dariiq, inkiis, bayaad, ximre, cuqle,* etc all these words are currently somewhat extinct in the spoken and written Somali.

---

[1] Xaydho, this term refers to the fat that covers the stomach of the goats. This fat was used in the past by the Somalis for telling the future. It was removed from the goat and held to the light. Conclusions were then drown from looking at the inside of the fat – about the weather, wars, rain, etc

3.1.3 Traditional Somali Herbal Medicine

Another area in which Muuse Galaal researched and wrote about during his time was traditional Somali herbal medicine and the trees which Somalis traditionally used for medicinal purposes, for example *Wancad, Waxaro-waalis, Gunre, Ridhmo, Dareemo, Sarin, Kariiri* and *Goror-kana* which are all trees of different sizes which were used for stopping blood loss from wounds. [15] While *Jaleelada, Xabag-xaddida, Dacar-biyoodda* and *Bogox-u-jeeddu* are trees which were used to treat constipation.

3.1.4 Language and writing the Somali Language

Muuse Galaal initially supported writing the Somali language in the Arabic alphabets with slight modifications, indeed he spent time in London getting a personalised typewriter made which could potentially write the modified Arabic form [17]. Muuse Galaal invented a form of written Somali, which consisted of modified Arabic alphabets with additional letters to account for the spoken Somali language. However, in the end and as the head of the committee responsible for forming a consensus on the written Somali language, Muuse Galaal supported writing the Somali language in the Latin alphabets. This became the consensus in the end and the Latin alphabet was used for the standardisation of written Somali. Much has been written about Muuse Galaal's advocacy for written Somali and his contribution to the written Somali language [17], [7], [10], [3].

3.2 Historian and collective memory collector

As a historian, Muuse Galaal tried his best to create a written record of the collective memory of the Somali speaking people. He collected stories and accounts of real historical events in the Horn of Africa both in his published books and other writings, and in his tape recordings. These materials have become the basic foundation for modern researchers. It has been narrated from Ali Sugulle "Duncarbeed" which says that Muuse Galaal use to say that Somali folk dance was exercise and this made it better than other forms of dance [4].

3.3 Poetry, sayings and poet

Muuse Galaal was a talented collector and preserver of Somali poetry, Somali culture, Somali sayings and phrases, as well as Somali stories, and worked hard to share this work with the wider population, through writing, presenting on the radio and giving public lectures [7]. He was a talented poet in his own right, and also wrote and directed several plays including "Qayb Libaax" (The Lion's Share), as well as around fifty original poems including "Hengel" (Mourning Cloth). Some of the written text that has been preserved from the thread of poems known as *Guba* are written in English. These poems which Muuse Galaal and Andrzejewski collaborated on translating [1] have given many researchers a great opportunity to learn something about Somali poetry.

3.4 Wisdom

Muuse Galaal was a thoughtful and wise man. In his story "Faaliyahii la bilkaday" (A Soothsayer Tested) which is part of his book Xikmad Soomaali [10] published in 1956, and reported in this book, he illustrated how "The [Somali] folktale reveals the richness of the Somali language, the limitless creative imagination of the Somalis and their amazing philosophical insights" [5].

4. Conclusion:

The writing of poetry and transnational knowledge and translation of this into other languages contributes to enriching the wisdom and traditions of the communities in question, it also enriches world poetry and knowledge as a whole. This was the contribution of Muuse Galaal. It is a privilege that now, with his death only a matter of years ago, we are celebrating Somali music and poetry in London, with translation the theme of this year's Somali Week Festival.

Halla gabo xilkaagee,
Horta yaa Galaalow,
Magacaaga gudi kara,

Guulahaaga qarin kara,
Kutubtaada gubi kara?
Maxamed Ibraahin Warsame, Hadraawi [4].

5. Bibliography, Commentary and Muuse Galaal most famous published work

[1] Andrzejewski, B.W. and M.H.I. Galaal (Muuse Xaaji Ismaaciil Galaal), *A Somali Poetic Combat,* Journal of African Languages, 1963.

[2] Andrzejewski, B. W. And Musa H.I.Galaal, *The art of the verbal message in Somali society,* in Lukas, Johannes (ed.), *Neue Afrikanistiche Studien,* Hamburger Beitrage zur Afrika-Kunde, 5, 1966, pp. 29-39.

[3] B. W. Andrzejewski, *Muuse Xaaji Ismaaciil Galaal (1914-1980): a founding father of written Somali,* Horn Of Africa, No.2, Vol 4. 1982. pp. 21-25.

[4] Cabdiraxmaan Faarax "Barwaaqo", *Mahadhadii Muuse Xaaji Ismaaciil Galaal,* Dhaxalreeb III, 2005, Ponte Invisbile, Pisa.

[5] Georgi Kapchits, *The Traveller to the Legendary Lands,* WardheerNews interview with Sheila Andrzejewski.

[6] Jaamac Muuse Jaamac, *Waraysiyo kala duwan eheladii Muuse Ismaaciil Galaal iyo dad kale.* 2011.

[7] Martin Orwin (contributed article) *Galaal, Muuse Xaaji Ismaaciil* in *Encyclopedia of African Literature,* Taylor and Francis, 2009.

[8] Muuse Xaaji Ismaaciil Galaal, *Terminology and practice of Somali Weather lore, Astronomy and Astrology,* published by the author, Mogadishu, May 1968.

[9] Muuse Xaaji Ismaaciil Galaal, *Stars, seasons and whether in Somali pastoral traditions,* Mogadishu, 1970.

[10] Muuse Haaji Ismaaciil Galaal. *Hikmad Soomaali.* Edited with grammatical introduction and notes by. B.W. Andrzejewski. London: Oxford University Pres. 1956.

[11] Muuse Haaji Ismaaciil Galaal. *Qaalle adduun,* qoraaga ayaa daabaay, Muqdishu, 1953.

[12] Muuse Haaji Ismaaciil Galaal. *Some observations on Somali culture* in *Perspectives on Somalia*, Somali Institute of Public Administration, Muqdishu, 1968, pp. 39-55.

[13] Musa H. I. Galaal, *A collection of Somali literature: Mainly from Sayid Mohamed Abdille Hassan*, Mogadishu, 1964.

[14] Muusa H. I. Galaal, *Some aspects of the Somalia pastoral medicine - notes*, Mogadishu, 19??.

[15] *Muuse Galaal. Seeska Hiddaha Soomaalida*, Muqdishu, 1969.

[16] *Musa Galaal. The Role of Oral tradition in the Somali Culture*, in *The Proceedings of the First International Congress of Somali Studies*, edited by Hussein M. Adam and Charles Lee Geshekter, Scholers Press, 1992.

[17] Galaal, Muuse H. I. *Arabic script for Somali*, in *Islamic Quarterly* 1/2, 1954, pp. 114-118.

[18] Tom Smoyer and Muusa H. I. Galaal, *Baadiye iyo beled*, Nairobi, Kenya: English Press, c.1969.

MUUSE GALAAL'S CONTRIBUTION TO THE ACADEMIC STUDY OF SOMALI LANGUAGE AND CULTURE.

Martin Orwin

Muuse Galaal's contribution to the academic study of Somali language and culture is very important both as an independent scholar and through his collaboration with B.W. Andrzejewski 'Guush'. Their collaboration began when Muuse was working as a teacher in the Department of Education of the then British Protectorate of Somaliland. Guush, with his wife Sheila, arrived in Sheekh in 1950 to undertake research on the Somali language under a Colonial Welfare and Development Research Scheme with a view to developing a script for the language which might then be officially used in the Protectorate. As such he began working with Muuse and developed a detailed knowledge of various aspects of the language. This close collaboration between the Western scholar trained in linguistics and phonetics (at the School of Oriental and African Studies, SOAS) along with the knowledgeable mother-tongue speaker of the language was an ideal way of undertaking such detailed linguistic investigation and the outcome was some seminal articles by Andrzejewski on the phonology, morphology and syntax of Somali. Although the script which Muuse and Guush developed was not taken up by the administration given local opposition to using the Latin alphabet, the work both scholars undertook was fundamental to subsequent discussion of writing Somali and many features were also retained in the subsequent official script developed by Shire Jaamac Axmed for the language which was introduced in 1972. These include the use of digraphs for long vowels and geminate consonants, the use of 'kh' for the voiceless uvular fricative and the 'q' for the uvular stop. Following this work Guush returned to the UK to work at SOAS and Muuse followed him there to take up a post as Research Assistant in Somali and to study phonetics. Given his work on the writing of Somali it is interesting to note that in 1954 he published a little known article in the *Islamic Quarterly* (Vol.1 No.2, pp.114-118) entitled 'Arabic Script for Somali', in which he presents his own script based on the Arabic alphabet for the writing of Somali language. This involves the use of some special letters to deal with the fact that the Arabic alphabet doesn't allow for all of the sounds of the Somali language, specifically the five short and five long vowels. His engagement with the writing of Somali continued following independence as a member of the later Somali Language Commission of which he was also for a time the chairman.

Aside from his linguistic work, Muuse was also a documenter of Somali oral literature both poetry and folktales as well as the traditional knowledge of the Somalis. During his time in London he prepared a collection of folktales written in the version of the Latin script that he and Andrzejewski had developed and with copious grammatical notes by Andrzejewski. This was published by Oxford University Press in 1956 as *Hikmad Soomaali* (the barred 'h' in the title is of course what is now written with 'x'), to this day it remains an important publication and is a useful tool for learning not just something of the rich folkloric heritage of the Somalis but also for understanding the language of these tales and the way the grammar is used. As Guush states in the Editor's Preface: 'Mr Galaal helped me, here in London, to prepare the Notes, particularly by explaining to me the more difficult words and idioms and those apsects of the Somali cultural background with which I was not familiar'. The grammar notes aside, the book is very much the work of Muuse and includes three poems which he composed especially for the stories. These along with the style of language used in the stories which is based on Muuse's experience of being immersed in the verbal culture of the Somali nomadic-pastoralist society mean that they, as Guush points out: 'bear a clear imprint of his [Muuse's] personality'. The presentation of these stories remains exemplary both in terms of the language, the way the language is presented (the careful attention to spelling for example) and the grammatical and cultural notes.

It was of course not only folktales, Muuse also collected a huge amount of poetry, some of which he transcribed and made into a collection and was printed in Mogadishu in 1964 as *A Collection of Somali Literature: Mainly from Sayid Mohamed Abdille Hassan*, a copy of which is in the special collection of SOAS. This is one of the earliest collections dedicated specifically to Somali poetry to have been printed and shows the foresight that Muuse had in terms of the documentation and preservation of the Somali literary heritage for the future. His knowledge and appreciation of poetry is also evident in another collaboration with Guush namely 'A Somali Poetic Combat' (*Journal of African Languages*, 2, pp.15-28, 93-100 & 190-205, 1963). This work is in three parts and provides the texts and translations of three of the first poems of the *Guba* chain of poems, those by Cali Dhuux, Qammaan Bulxan and Salaan Carrabey. This is a work that could only have come about through collaboration and is again an exemplary presentation of Somali poetry to a readership who have no experience of this. The texts are interesting in terms of the script used since they introduce the use of some letters which eventually found their way into the official script. 'dh' is used for the retroflex plosive instead of the previous tailed 'd' and 'c' is used for the voiced pharyngeal fricative; there is also a change from the barred 'h' to using 'ch' instead. Following an introduction to work on Somali poetry and the way the language is written the authors provide a historical and social background to the poems. This is a feature of all of Andrzejewski's work on Somali poetry and the knowledge Muuse brings to this is invaluable and indeed will no doubt have contributed to further work published by Andrzjewski on his own. The translations precede the Somali texts in the articles and copious notes are given with reference to particular lines and groups of lines. The translations are sensitive not only with respect to reflecting the original language accurately, but also in terms of the English language used. It is important to bear in mind here that Guush often pointed out that in his translation work, his wife Sheila always helped. As a native

Polish speaker Guush recognized the contribution that could be made by having a native English speaker look through the translations. This work is one of only a few in depth descriptions and presentations of individual poems in Somali and is a testament to the collaboration between the two scholars.

Another very important work of Muuse Galaal is *Seeska Hiddaha Soomaalida* (The Basic Traditional Education of the Somalis) which was printed in 1969 and comprises poetry, proverbs and tales and items of vocabulary relating to various topics such as knowledge, respect for parents, leadership as well as the lunar stations, traditional names of the months etc. This is a rich collection and an important record of the knowledge of a scholar who had the foresight to write this down at the time. In the following year (1970) he expanded on the traditional knowledge of astronomy, weather and the seasons with the printing of *Stars, Seasons and Weather in Somali Pastoral Traditions* which remains the most comprehensive account of this part of traditional knowledge of the Somalis (a copy of this was deposited in the library of the SOAS). In this work, written in English, Muuse sets out in detail the knowledge which he himself had and that which he gathered from many elders whom he acknowledges along with Guush and I.M. Lewis and also John Johnson who helped with a preliminary report on the weather lore. In this he uses a system for writing Somali in which the voiceless pharyngeal fricative, the 'x', is written in yet another way namely as a digraph 'hh'. The work is undoubtedly the most important of its type relating to Somali traditional knowledge of the environment and deserves a wider readership (this has been helped by it being part of a compilation of works on Somali folklore made by David Hunt entitled *Somalia: Miscellaneous Folklore* (2006), copies of which have been deposited in the SOAS library and the British Library). The detail in which Muuse describes this knowledge and the way he associates this with the life of the people is exemplary. The stations of the moon for example are presented in a systematic manner which includes the meaning of the name, the stars associated with it, the associated weather and also the astrological significance.

Muuse Galaal's legacy in the field of Somali cultural and literary studies is a lasting one not only given the work he wrote himself but also given the collaborations he made with Somali elders and Western scholars. We have much to be thankful for in the contributions he made and it is to be hoped that his work finds its way to the younger generation of Somalis, particularly those growing up away from the Horn who may have a limited idea of their rich cultural heritage.

A SOOTHSAYER TESTED

By Musa Ismail Galaal translated by Georgi Kapchits and
edited by Sheila Andrzejewski

Once upon a time there was a soothsayer who was good at telling
fortunes with his beads. Everybody loved him, and if anything
happened to a man he would go and ask him to tell his fortune,
which he did. And when a Somali soothsayer tells somebody's
fortune he does not say: 'It will be so and so' but he says: 'In
olden times they used to say so and so.'

All the people loved that soothsayer and used to come to him
from everywhere, so that soon he was famous all over the country.
At last the news about him reached the sultan himself, and
hearing how the people praised the man he said to himself: 'You
must check whether his skill is really so great.' So one day when
the soothsayer was mentioned in his presence the sultan said:

'In my opinion he doesn't know how to do anything extraordinary!'
But in response he was told:
'Sultan, nobody ever met a wiser man than he!'
Then the sultan said:
'Well then, bring him to me and I'll put a question to him. If he
answers it, then he is wise indeed and I'll reward him, but if not – he
is a cheat and I'll order his head to be cut off!'
The people were alarmed and said:
'Sultan, he is a very good man – don't execute him!'
In reply the sultan said:
'Find him and bring to me.'
Then people were sent out with the order:
'You have seven days for the search.'

After a time the people who had been sent out found the
soothsayer and brought him to the sultan, who convoked a

council. When all had arrived, the sultan addressed the soothsayer with the following words:

'Listen, was it you who convinced the people of your wisdom?'
The soothsayer took fright and thought: 'This is obviously going to turn out badly for me.' So he said to the sultan:
'No, it wasn't me.'
The sultan laughed and said:
'Stop that - they say all over the country: "This man is very wise!" Well then, if that's so you must answer the question I'm going to ask you.'

The soothsayer lost heart and stood there in embarrassment, unable to utter a word. Then all those who were present said to the sultan:

'O Sultan, we know this man, he's a true sage – ask him your question!'
The sultan got angry and said to him:
'What, you answer the questions of others and don't want to answer mine?'
The soothsayer said:
'No, Sultan, I have no wisdom.'
Then the sultan ordered him:
'Do whatever you want, tell fortunes by beads or by leaves, but you must tell me what will happen to us during the coming year! And you had better know that if your prediction comes true, you'll get a great deal of livestock as a reward, but if not – I'll give the order to behead you.'

The soothsayer took out his beads and started to count them over, and in this way he made calculations for a long time. But in the end the beads foretold a disaster for him. Gripped by fear he threw the beads on the ground and began to shout curses. Then he ran to the beads, seized them with his teeth and bit two of them right off. After that he was not able to stop himself and grasping a dagger he cut off his finger – slash, slash. Blood gushed and gushed from the wound, and those who witnessed what he had done were amazed and said: 'He has gone mad, beware of his dagger!' Then the sultan ordered:

'Speak out!'

The soothsayer replied:

'Sultan, I won't tell you what was predicted. The beads foretold a misfortune for me, but I myself magicked it away.'

The sultan said:

'So tell the fortune again!'

The soothsayer took up the beads again and showed the sultan what had turned out.

The sultan asked:

'And what does it mean?'

The man counted the beads once more and they predicted 'a long way'. Overcome by fright he dropped them.

'What's happened?' asked the sultan, for the soothsayer was standing with his mouth open, unable to utter a word.

Then the sultan ordered:

'Reveal what has come out!'

The man could only mumble:

'Sultan, O Sultan...'

Seeing that he was unable to say anything the sultan moved towards him and demanded:

'Say something for heaven's sake!'

But the man said

'O Sultan, my skill has betrayed me.'

Now the sultan was angry and with the words 'On the seventh day I'll be expecting answer to my question!', let him go. The sultan retired and the rest of the people began to disperse.

The soothsayer waited till they had gone away then once again picked up the beads. He began to count them, but they came up with nonsense and he hurled them away and fell to cursing divination. He walked back and forth talking to himself, out of his mind and deep in darkness. He began talking deliriously, but after a while he came to his senses, recovered a little from his fear and said to himself: 'You fool, listen! It can't go on like this – collect yourself, drive away your fear and get down to fortune-telling in the proper way.' He started to tell his beads again, but – alas! – again a meaningless set came out. He counted again – the result was the same. He realised that now things were looking bad, but what could be done? He thought and thought, then stood up and said:

'O Lord, I swear that till I find the answer I won't sleep, eat or talk to anybody, and I won't go near people at all!'

The soothsayer went to a deserted area covered with bushes. He walked and walked, moving further and further away from any place with people. He would sit down under a tree and count his beads, from which again nothing would come out, while sometimes he would cut off the leaves of plants and divine from them, getting no answer from them either. At last he broke down altogether, stopped under a big shady tree and thought: 'Well, if you're finished, stay here and may death find you under this very tree.' He put down his prayer mat and settled himself under the tree.

He spent several days there, and every daybreak and every nightfall he would stand up, take his beads and count them for a long time in the hope that his prophetic gift would come back to him. But time and again a meaningless set would turn out.

At last it was only one day short of the appointed date and he was full of dismal presentiments, having decided that he was destined to die in that very place. But from the roots of the tree in whose shadow he was lying there came creeping a serpent, old and of great size. He sprang to his feet, grasped his spear, ran to one side, then turned towards the serpent and said to himself: 'Be all eyes!' But the serpent coiled itself into a ball, stuck out its head and addressed him with the following words:

'Why did you run away?'

He answered:

'You frightened me and I must be on the alert!'

Then the serpent said:

'Don't be afraid of me – I won't do you any harm. I want to talk to you.'

Now the soothsayer, who had never before seen a serpent speaking a human language, was so amazed that he did not even understand what the serpent had said, and he raised his hands to his head in wonder. Then he said:

'I can't believe you – I've never seen a talking serpent before!'

The serpent laughed and said:
'Well, you hadn't seen one before, but you see one now!'
The soothsayer said:
'I don't trust you.'
The serpent answered:
'We can make an agreement.'

The soothsayer was silent for a while, but then agreed. Now the serpent stretched out the end of its tail, hard as horn, and with it drew a big circle on the ground. Then it went to the centre of the circle and swore: 'Wallaahi, Billaahi, Tallaahi, I swear by God that I won't do you any harm unless you yourself force me to it.' Having said this, it left the circle.

Now the soothsayer stepped into the circle and swore too. The oaths finished, they talked in a friendly fashion about one thing and another. Then the serpent asked:
'Why did you come to this land? What are you looking for?'
He answered:
'I'm a soothsayer. My sultan ordered me to foretell what will happen next year, but my skill betrayed me. Then I came here to go on with my divination.'
The serpent asked:
'Did you find the answer?'
'No.'
'What if I prompt you with the answer?' asked the serpent. 'What reward can you offer me?'
'Demand anything you want!'
The serpent said:
'And what reward will you receive if you answer the sultan's question correctly?'
'The sultan promised me a lot of livestock.'
'Well', said the serpent, 'if I foretell what will happen next year, do you agree to give me half the livestock you will receive from the sultan?'
'I swear by God,' exclaimed the soothsayer, 'that everything I get will be yours!'
The serpent said:
'Why everything? Half will be yours and half mine.'

'I agree,' said the soothsayer.

Then the serpent said:

'Deliver to the sultan the following message[2]:

"I have found out the secrets of the time that is to come

Listen to what I have to say!

Eight years have passed since the deeds of Ibliis, Prince of Evil.

The round of the years has brought back the jinns

And all their wicked deeds.

There are signs to be seen in the return of this eighth year –

A wife who covers her head with a mourning-scarf,

Brave men slaughtered, looted herds,

Vultures pecking at the flesh of sturdy warriors,

Disaster!

Men are preparing busily for war,

Their rusty battle-spears made newly sharp.

Horses are fattened, and harnessed ready for the tray.

And once-dry waterskins, with fastening new-fixed,

Are ready again to slake men's thirst.

Whether you close your eyes in sleep, whether you flee,

Or whether in readiness you draw your sword from its scabbard,

Soon there will come a fierce and determined cohort

And against the very dust the encounter with them raises

You will cry out to God in awe!'"

No sooner had the soothsayer listened to the end of the *geeraar*[3] than he sprang to his feet, blessed the serpent and hurried off to the sultan. Meanwhile the people of his settlement had gathered and they said:

'The time is running out, but the soothsayer hasn't come yet. Where is he?'

Some answered:

'Probably he hasn't found the answer and is hiding somewhere.'

---

[2] This and two other predictions of the serpent were put into verse by Muuse Xaaji Ismaaciil Galaal. Translated into English by B.W. Andrzejewski and Sheila Andrzejewski (An Anthology of Somali Poetry. Bloomington-Indianapolis, 1993).

[3] Somali poetic genre the theme of which is usually war, challenge to single combat etc.

Others said:

'Yes, today is the last day, but let's wait till evening.'

In the afternoon they saw in the distance a cloud of dust and asked each other:

'What might this mean?'

Then they saw a man who was running and singing – it was the soothsayer. His lips were shrunken and cracked, his body emaciated, his eyes sunken. No wonder – he had not had a scrap of food in his mouth for seven days. How ill he looked!

The soothsayer, as is proper, first went up to the sultan and shook his hand. Then, with the people standing round and holding their breath, he performed the *geeraar* he had learnt from the serpent. Now, with their hearts jumping for joy, they came running up to the soothsayer and started to shake his hand. And the sultan said:

'Take him to my house and slaughter for him a really fat she-camel.'

The sultan sent out the heralds with the order to round up all his subjects with the message: 'In eight days' time we are having a general council and everybody must come.'

On the eighth day the whole tribe to a man came together for a council. The sultan said:

'A time of war is coming. Each one of you must feed his horse, take his weapon and sharpen his spear. The horses must be kept in readiness. Until the war starts we'll be assembling here every day.'

This they did, and every day they assembled, made ready their weapons for the battle, sent out patrols and did not return home at night to sleep. And one day the patrols sent them a message: 'Arise, we're being attacked!'

All the men jumped on their horses and grasped their swords and spears. And early in the morning, when the livestock had been driven to pasture, a tramping and whooping horde swooped down. But because the tribe had been warned beforehand and were ready for the battle, their warriors were able to make a surprise attack on the enemy, repulsed their attack, put them to flight and chased them away.

A while later another detachment attacked the settlement and was crushed. The time of wars had come, and there were battles every morning and every night. The light went dark and the people forgot about sleep and rest. The tribe defeated all the enemies who had invaded its land and all its campaigns were successful because everything had been foreseen in advance.

A year went by in this way, and all the tribes except the one ruled by the sultan were destroyed in the wars.

One day the sultan summoned his tribe and made a speech in which he paid tribute to each of his warriors. Then, addressing the soothsayer, he said:

'You have done good work and I am satisfied with you. As a token of gratitude, accept from me a herd of camels, a herd of sheep and goats, a herd of cattle and a herd of horses.'

The soothsayer rejoiced, thanked the sultan and took the animals that had been presented to him.

As he drove away his livestock he suddenly recollected his agreement with the serpent, and said to himself: 'You must drive them to the serpent and give it its share.' But when he looked at his precious livestock, greediness stirred in him and he said to himself: 'Are you really going to give these beautiful animals to the serpent? You're a fool and the son of a fool! Instead of giving such possessions to that beast you'd better take your sword and be done with it at one stroke!' He drew his sword out of its sheath, entrusted his servants with the care of the animals and set off in search of the serpent.

He found it sleeping in its usual place. He raised his sword and said to himself: 'Cut off its head!' But at the very moment he said to himself: 'Strike!' the serpent woke up, dashed towards some bushes and slithered away to safety. The sword hit the place where the serpent's head had been lying. Now the soothsayer said to himself: 'May your hand wither and fall off! Now if it jumps on you out of the bush you'll have to run away, going all out!' And he started running with all his might – he was off like a shot. He ran and ran without a backward glance till he reached the livestock he had left under his servants' supervision, and started hurrying them too, shouting:

'Save the livestock!'

Together with his people he drove the animals away and they did not stop until they found themselves in a safe place.

One day, after a long time had passed since the soothsayer had returned home, and when he had had a good rest and was enjoying his life, some messengers came from the sultan and said: 'The sultan has sent us to bring you to him.'

'What does he need me for?'

'We don't know,' was the answer.

'Well, well' muttered the soothsayer, shaking his head. He was silent as he thought for a while, asking himself: 'I wonder what the sultan wants from me now?' Then he stood up and followed the messengers.

They walked and walked until at last they came to the sultan, who was sitting among his advisers. He rejoiced when he saw the soothsayer, shook his hand and asked how he was getting on. After a while he asked:

'Do you know why I've called you? Last year you saved us all when you predicted what was going to happen. Now I want you to tell us what the next year will bring.'

The frightened soothsayer hung his head. Then he asked:

'Was this what you called me for?'

'Yes.'

'O Sultan,' he answered. 'Don't you remember that my skill betrayed me?'

But the sultan answered:

'No, may God be the witness, it didn't betray you, since last year your prediction came true, so don't say what nobody is going to believe! Go, move away for seven days like you did last year, then come back and reveal what's going to happen next year. Let the agreement between us be the same as before.'

Now the soothsayer realised that things were looking bad. What was to be done? While he was sitting there lost in thought the people departed and he was left alone. At the crack of dawn he was still sitting there, engrossed in thought.

'What if I go to the serpent with remorse and apologies,' he thought, 'and say: "Listen – forgive me, for I treated you badly before. And now I'm in the same awful situation as I was then.

Help me again, please!"' And he decided to do this and went running to the serpent. He found it lying in the same place, and started repentantly to weep, saying:

'Listen, O serpent – I dealt with you in a very bad way. I alone am to be blamed, for I violated our agreement, but I beg you to forgive me and help me to get out of the trouble I've got into again!'

The serpent laughed and said:

'Oh, you clearly proved yourself, and it seems it was God's will to keep me alive. As for you, you did everything you could to finish me, but there is nothing to be done about that. Not without reason they say: "Unless people forget the evil done to them it will not rain.[4]" In the name of God I'll help you, so listen what I'm going to tell you:

'Mankind, O Diviner, was destined, it seems,
To be the cause of this world's woes.
Butchering each other was *your* invention
'Stab' was a word that *you* devised,
And the fire that you have kindled
Will consume a large part of creation.
When you are weak and defenceless
How fond you are of friendship
And the support of mutual aid –
But for the man you called your friend
When you were pressed by need,
You care nothing when your purpose is achieved!

You have broken the covenant into which you entered
And the pact that once was made between us.
The evil deeds of the sons of Adam
Will surely end by destroying the world!
What you say out loud with your lips
You do not really mean in your heart.

It was I who saved you from a trap
When you came to me in such dire straits.

---

[4] A Somali proverb.

I expected some reward from you
But instead, you dolt, the profit I gained
Was a deadly blow from a hilted sword!
The thud and crack of that sword of yours –
The cloud of dust that vexed my head –
The fear in which I fled from you –
Leaping, stumbling, dashing against euphorbia trees –
My ears were made deaf by all that happened!
O how I was taken in by you –
By that trickling tear, that gaunt aspect,
Those pleading words which touched my flesh,
Those jinn-like supplications!

So do not look for trust from me
For that trust fell down a very deep hole.
I shall tell you this, for the sake of God –
You are a doer of evil deeds!
I have no doubt that many a time
You have oppressed weak men and orphans.

And in my view you are paying now
For all the injustice you committed –
An old debt of yours is now being settled.

Nevertheless – tell the sultan who sent you here
That a wasting drought will come.
Tell him the grass in the pastures will wither,
That trees will die, the ones that stand in groves
And the ones that grow alone and tall.
Tell him that water will no longer flow
In pool or shallow well, valley or running stream.
Tell him that those who are weak and poor
Will perish with their flocks
And only the black-headed sheep
And the sturdiest camels will live.
But tell him, too, that hard work and resourcefulness
Will help a man to survive till the rains return.'
Hearing this the soothsayer jumped for joy, spinning round and
round, and said:

'Oh serpent, I remember how I treated you then, but this time I'll reward you for all you did for me. Be sure that what happened won't happen again. I'll give you everything I get, I promise.'
'Well, we shall see,' said the serpent.
The soothsayer set off and ran and ran till he reached his settlement. He performed the gabay[5] he had learnt from the serpent, and when he had finished the people rejoiced and rushed to him to lift him up. The sultan, pleased, stood up, shook his hand and patted his head as a sign of benevolence. All the people began to glorify the soothsayer and held festivities in his honour. The next day the sultan summoned his tribe and said:
'A year of severe drought has been predicted for us, therefore everyone must keep something in reserve.' And everyone made a special shelf for storing food and they were all the time putting something aside there.

Several months later a drought started. It did not rain in autumn and it did not rain in spring. Clouds of dust were flying everywhere, the earth turned into a desolate wilderness, the trees dried up and there was no water anywhere. Only in the deepest underground wells did a little water remain, but the shallow wells were dry. And then all the cattle and other domestic animals died, for they could not go without water for long, and only the sturdiest camels survived. All the other tribes which had not got ready for the drought perished, together with their livestock, and only the sultan and his tribe held out with what they had stored, and survived that difficult time.

The sultan called the soothsayer again and gave him a great number of animals. The soothsayer rejoiced and drove them to his encampment. But on the way he remembered his agreement with the serpent. He stopped his herds, sat down and started to draw on the ground. He sat and thought for a long time, then raised his head and looked at the animals which were grazing round him. Now it is known that greediness is an awful thing, and it stirred in him again.

---

[5] The most important poetic genre, dealing with serious subjects, generally about 30-150 lines in length.

And he told himself: 'Are you really going to cast all these animals into the throat of the serpent which is now lying there in the shadow? You are a fool, the son of a fool!' But then he recollected himself suddenly and thought: 'Yes, but you made a promise to the serpent, and not to fulfil a promise is just the same as not believing in God[6]. What's to be done?' But then he said: 'I swear by the name of God, the camels and the other animals are mine and I'll take them for myself, come what may!' And he drove the livestock away and once again did not keep his word.

One day, when the drought was still raging, the sultan's messengers visited the soothsayer and said:

'The sultan has ordered you to come quickly.'

The soothsayer thought: 'Oh God, what does he want me for this time?' He was scared, but did not dare disobey the order and went to the sultan with his messengers.

So they came to the sultan who was sitting with his advisers. The sultan and the soothsayer shook hands, sat down and talked about one thing and another, and then the sultan said:

'Listen, I called you for one thing, which is easy for you and very important for us.'

The soothsayer was frightened.

'What is it, sultan?' he asked.

'This year and the previous one, twice indeed, you saved us from great disasters. Those who had not been forewarned perished in last year's war or this year's drought. As for us, thanks to you and to God, both people and livestock are safe and sound. Therefore we want you once more to predict the coming year.'

'To predict what?' The horror-stricken soothsayer jumped high into the air, lost consciousness and fell to the ground.

In a fit of anger the sultan sprang to his feet and with the words 'Every time I ask him to be of service to us he dares to be displeased and angry!' he raised his whip, but the people who were standing nearby took it away from him. Then he said:

'When this rascal comes to himself tell him that if I don't receive the answer in three days he will feel my sword!'

---

[6] A Somali proverb.

The people stood for a long time over the soothsayer and when he finally came to his senses they told him the sultan's words. He understood that things were looking bad and said to himself: 'You can't allow yourself to be seen by the serpent, but if you don't find the answer you'll find death.' Then he asked himself: 'What is there left for me to do? If you go to the serpent, what will it say? Oh well, let it say whatever it wants. It's all the same – I'm going to the serpent.' And he ran off to find it.

'Hallo!' laughed the snake when it saw him. 'Is it me you are looking for?'

'It is you,' answered the soothsayer.

'And what do you want from me?' asked the serpent.

He replied:

'I've got the same question.'

Then the serpent said:

'Tell the sultan who sent you here
That the sky will bring back the clouds once more
For it is barren no longer, and carries the Dirir[7] rains.
Tell him that soon, on a night half-spent,
Flashes of lightning will be seen,
And the bountiful plenty of the Daydo rains
Will fall, just as it used to do.
Tell him that showers will pass over the land
That had been laid bare by drought.
Tell him that the herds will suffer no more
On their long treks to the water-holes.
Tell him that torrents will scurry like lizards
Through the dry scrub of arid valleys,
That fresh grass will spring up round the encampments
And that among the herds that have survived the drought
There will be beasts in milk.

Tell him that the wife who was banished from her husband's side
In the rigorous months of the rainless season
Will soon build a hut as spacious as a house of stone.

---

[7] Name of a bright star.

Now she can put off her workaday clothes
And dress herself anew in the silks
She had kept rolled up against this time.
Incense-burners appear from nooks and crannies
And a mat for sleeping is spread in a snug recess.
For her husband had had no thought of love
While the harsh dry season lasted,
But now that his flesh has lost its gauntness
He will come once more inside the hut.
Now he can choose what food he will eat –
No longer is he driven by hunger alone.
Over and over, with tender little words, he will be asked
To take more, and yet again more.
His wife will come and go, fetching this bowl or that,
And as she passes to and fro so close to him
The love that had grown old will become young again,
And in their revelry and play sons of blessing
Will be conceived, sons bright as thunderbolts.

Tell the sultan, too, that the younger men
Will not remain for long unwed.
They will marry, in a befitting way,
The girls they have been yearning for,
And riding displays and dancing
Will entertain and honour them.
And tell him, finally, that a man who so wishes
Will be free to turn his mind to faith and prayer.'

The soothsayer immediately rushed to the sultan and related
everything. And again he was thanked as before, and even more.

And soon after this, towards evening, a small cloud appeared far
away in the east. The people cried out:
'It's a cloud, by God!'
Nevertheless nobody thought that the small cloud could betoken
rain. But no sooner had the livestock been driven into the
enclosures than lightning flashed in the east. Everybody was
happy, the women were ululating gaily. God be praised, there
was nothing to be worried about any more. Before the people

had time to look around somebody said:
'God be praised, that cloud's already overhead!'
Somebody else said:
'Let's dig drainage ditches and get the weak animals to shelter!'
The people did so, and after all the houses had been dug around
with ditches and the livestock had been protected, they fell asleep.
Now, God be thanked, after a quarter of the night had passed it
started to rain, pitter-patter, pitter-patter. After exactly as much
water as was needed had fallen on the ground the rain stopped.
Then the animals were turned out to drink from the puddles and
the people stocked up with some water. At daybreak it rained
again and the livestock was driven out to grass. It rained four
days in succession and all the animals – camels, sheep and goats
– drank their fill, and even those which had no milk during the
drought began to give it. All the people drank as much milk as
they wanted.

In the middle of spring the sultan summoned his tribe and settled
all the disputes which had arisen during the drought. Having
finished with this he called the soothsayer and gave him many
animals of every kind.

Now the soothsayer said to himself: 'God be my witness, three
times the serpent saved you from misfortune and twice you
violated the agreement. This time you must keep your word, show
your gratitude and hand over to the serpent all the animals you
have received today as a reward.' And so he did. He drove all his
animals to the serpent and said:
'Oh serpent, I want to say to you three things. First of all, twice
when you helped me I returned you evil for good, but I repent of
what I did. Here are the animals I have received today – take
them all and forgive me! Secondly, I beg you to become my friend.
Finally, as I see that your wisdom is limitless, I ask you to tell me
about the world and about life!'
In answer the serpent said:
'As for friendship – I become a friend to no one. I either harm a
man or help him, according to the purpose for which I have been
sent.

As for forgiveness – I have forgiven you. As for the animals you brought to me – I give them all back into your hands, but nevertheless I regard the gift as having been accepted.

Now as for the world and life – I tell you this: world there is, but life is not distinct from it. Your life, as you call it, goes as the world goes, for God made the world with many patterns and it is these that rule men's lives. When war is the pattern of the times all men are at enmity with each other, and thus it was that in the war just past you took your sword against me even after I had helped you, and said to yourself, "Cut off his head!" And then again, at a time of drought no man is generous to his fellows, so you ran away with all your herds, giving me no share in the sultan's reward. But when there is a pattern of prosperity, what man is ever niggardly or full of hate? So you came to me, offering me all you had, not keeping even one animal for yourself. Each time it was the pattern, not yourself, that forced you to do whatever you did.

And now I shall tell you who I am. I am not a serpent, but Fate, the Leveller, and you will not see me again after this day – farewell!

ARABIC SCRIPT FOR SOMALI

M. H. I. Galaal

The Somalis, who inhabit the Horn of Africa and speak a language considered to belong to the Cushitic group of the Hamitic family, have been Muslims for several centuries. In all matters connected with Islam they use Arabic: they pray in Arabic and their learned men use Arabic in the study and application of Muslim law and theology. Also in other domains of life Arabic is used in a way reminiscent of the use of Latin in medieval Europe. Yet the majority of the Somali people are only superficially acquainted with this language: to learn Arabic well is a question of a good many years of full-time schooling. In contrast, a Somali can become literate in his own language in a fairly short time and without any great difficulty. With the advent of education on a large scale and with the growing need for responsible literate citizens, the problem of writing Somali has become very important.

Until now there has been no generally accepted script for the Somali language. Several attempts have been made by Somalis and Europeans alike in the past, but none of them has been successful for one reason or other. Sayid Mohamed Abdilla Hassan, and Mohamed Abdi Makahil, also a Somali, have used the Arabic script, and a similar attempt was made by Captain J. S. King in his two articles on 'Somali as a Written Lanuguage' in 1887.

The chief technical difficulty met by those early orthographers was the inadequacy of the Arabic vowel letters for writing down Somali. Arabic, owing to its structure, can be written with the omission of all the short vowels represented by the *harakat*, i.e. the vowel points. In Somali if the *harakat* were omitted the reader would have to guess the meaning from the context all the time, and this might not be possible in many cases. To use the *harakat* throughout would be impractical in everyday use, particularly as the Arabic *harakat* would have to be supplemented by at least two additional new signs.

There are two comparatively recent attempts which produced equally satisfactory ways of writing down Somali. These are the Roman transcription on phonetic principles devised by E. L. Armstrong and later modified by B. W. Andrzejewski of the School of Oriental and African Studies, University of London: the main principles of this transcription have been adopted by C. R. V. Bell, the late Director of Education, Somaliland Protectorate, in his recent book, *The Somali Language*; and the Somalia writing, previously known as Osmania; a description of this writing has been given by Professor Maino (see Bibliography). In spite of their great merits, neither of these two systems of transcription has much chance of winning great favour with the Somalis, on account of having no connexion with the Muslim world to which the Somalis belong, and neither of them has, in my opinion, the same educational value for the Somalis as the Arabic transcription.

Although the previous attempts to write down the Somali language in Arabic script have failed, the choice of using Arabic script for Somali was, and still is, obvious on practical grounds. A certain knowledge of Arabic is widespread among the Somalis in towns and in the interior alike. The Quranic Schools and the Itinerant Theological Schools *(hher)* have a long tradition in Somaliland, and have penetrated to the most remote parts of the interior. Moreover, the Arabic alphabet, not only the Arabic language, is a link common to many Muslim countries. Arabic printing-presses are easily accessible, and the cost of printing is, therefore, not very great. It is also my own opinion that any other script unfamiliar to the majority of Somalis is likely to create an exclusive class of literate men, in fact a ruling minority, and this might in the long run bring a great deal of unhappiness to Somaliland.

The system which I have presented here disposes of the difficulty in the Arabic vowel system. Here I have modified the Arabic vowel points by converting them into letters. These letters are somewhat reminiscent of the Arabic vowel points. The equivalent of *fatha* has an up-stroke, the equivalent of *kasra* a down-stroke, and the equivalent of *damma* has a rounded top. I have also invented four signs for the four Somali vowel sounds which do not exist in Arabic. I have not made any change in the principle of the use of the three long vowel letters already represented in Arabic by ا, و, ي, nor in the numerals.

This adaptation of the Arabic alphabet for Somali is entirely of my own invention, but the phonetic principles underlying it are based on the Roman transcription already mentioned. My transcription can easily be transliterated into, and from, both the Roman orthography and the Somalia writing. As a Somali who has the affairs of his country deep at heart, I put this adaptation of the Arabic script forward as a proposal, believing that it is suitable for our needs, and I beg my readers to consider it seriously and fairly.

Naturally the ultimate decision will rest with the Somalis themselves, who should give a fair trial to all the three existing systems and choose the best. The decision on the choice of an alphabet for our national orthography, naturally, can only be taken after discussions between the Somali public and the authorities concerned. In making their decision, however, the Somalis, with the help of their European administrators, should consider Somaliland, its economy, and its present and future position in the world. They should also realize that the Arabic script, already well established in our country, has the greatest chance of becoming a medium of rapid educational progress and the spreading of literacy.

Using the Arabic script for Somali would not mean abandoning the beautiful language of Islam. It would mean, I am sure, strengthening our bonds with Islam and the Muslim world, without causing inconvenience to ourselves by neglecting our own language, and would even help those Somalis who learn Arabic.

The outline of Arabic Script devised for Somali

The shape of the new signs in the various positions i.e :

Roman Characters | Corresponding Arabic characters | Characters devised for Somali

	Finally		Medially		Initially	
a	ل	la = قلد	bar = بر	ab = ابد
i	گ	si = سگ	lib = لب	ib = اب
u	گ	gu = تگ	tun = تن	ul = ال
e	3	se = سو	hel = هل	eg = اگ
o	ط	lo = لطی	col = عل	og = اگ
ee	×‌	gee = گلد	ceel = عل	eeg = اگ
oo	ٮ	too = تٮ	gool = گل	oog = اگ
	ں	This sign is added to any new final sign

Letters already used in Arabic transcription

Roman	Arabic	Somali		Roman	Arabic	Somali
aa	ى	ى		sh	ش	ش
ii	ي	ي		kh	خ	خ
uu	و	و		x	ح	ح
t	ت	ت		c	ع	ع
d	د	د		h	ه	ه
k	ك	ك		m	م	م
g	ق	ق		n	ن	ن
f	ف	ف		t	ل	ل
q	ق	ق		w	و	و
b	ب	ب		y	ي	ي

ماهماه = Proverb

١. وليان دينتى لمى داعلك لمدينهى دليدلى كلى حلاىا.
٢. هلقان فلرهى جمرهى فلممهى على جمرتى.
٣. علنان كلى ياب ىد رتر على دىجى.
٤. وليمى علملعشلى كتى جمرا علرزليلتى علمل.
٥. وايلل ذهبتيسلى كلمقتلى كتى لاسلى.
٦. ولى للميسكلى عجيملى بلا ملى كلنلى.
٧. بلرقشمى همرتعلا قلى نهعمى.
٨. ولعلى ملى ديمهى فى ولملى كلى شهشيملى دلى.
٩. جلمرهى هلاد بلى تلقلان.
١٠. وايللل وا ملنس ذلملللا.

Transliteration

1. wataan diinta ama daa'ad ahayai,
   dabaday ka kumaan.
2. haddaan fari jirin fahmo ma jirto
3. 'amaan ka yaab neer ma doojo.
4. wata 'aloosha ku jiraa 'aarabku kadaa.
5. waayeel fabtiisa kaftan ku laasay.
6. wat layska oggahay eed ma keeno.
7. barasho hortaad hay ni'in.
8. watan ka dejin e wata ka shisheeya day.
9. gari llah bay tagaan.
10. waayeel waa mud dambeed.

Translation

1. What is not godly & honest comes to a bad end.
2. Where there is no writing there is no memory.
3. Diffidence never succeeds.
4. What is in the heart steals the tongue.
5. Elders often end a serious talk with a jest.
6. When warning has been given there is no room for blame.
7. Don't hate me before you know me.
8. Don't look only at the things in front of you, look beyond them.
9. Justice obeys only God.
10. Elders protect you like an outer fence.

Bibliography

(a) Roman transcription

L.E. Armstrong, *"The Phonetic Structure of Somali"*, Mitteilungen des Seminars fur Orientalische Sprachen, xxxvii. 3. 1934, pp. 116-61.
G.R.V. Bell, *The Somali Language*. London, 1953 (Longmans, Green & Co.).

(b) Somalia writing

Mario Maino, *La Lingua Somala, Strumento* L'Insegnamento Professionale. Alessandria (Italy), 1953 (Tipografia Ferrari, Occella and Co.).
Mario Maino, *'L'Alfabeto "Osmania" in Somalia'*, Rassegna di Studi Etiopici, volume x, Genn.-Dic. 1951, pp. 99-107.

(c) Arabic transcription:

J.S. KING, 'Somali as a Written Language5, The Indian Antiquary, August 1887, pp. 242-3, and October 1887, pp. 285-7.

THE SOMALI TALE "A SOOTHSAYER TESTED"[1]

Alexander Zholkovsky

Despite the progress made in the creation of Somali written culture over the last 10-15 years[2], Somali remains a predominantly oral language. The number of the recorded pieces of verbal art is rather limited as regards both poetry, remarkable for its refined style, and folk prose, consisting mainly of short tales or anecdotes. The 'Soothsayer Tested'[3] stands out among these latter by its philosophical content and consummate artistic form. On three occasions prose narration is interrupted by 'acts' in verse[4]. All this makes 'The Soothsayer' a unique manifestation of Somali 'high prose', situated halfway between poems and regular folktales. Let us examine the tale's narrative and thematic structure.

1. The goals of the analysis

The plot of the tale is briefly as follows.

The sultan calls a famous soothsayer and orders him, on pain of death, to predict what will happen to his tribe in the coming year. The soothsayer tries fortune-telling by beads but his skill betrays him. He moves away from the people, continues his attempts but in vain. Suddenly a serpent

---

[1] This is a condensed version of the article published in Russian in the Russian-language journal Narody Azii i Afriki, 1 (Moscow, 1970).

[2] See *M.Moreno*, Il Somalo della Somalia, Roma, 1955; *M.Galaal, B.W.Andrzejewski,* Hikmad Soomaali, London, 1956; *B.W.Andrzejewski, Muusa Galaal,* A Somali Poetic Combat, Michigan, 1963; *B.W.Andrzejewski, I.M.Lewis,* Somali Poetry, Oxford, 1964; *Shire Jaamac Achmed,* Gabayo, maahmaah iyo sheekooyin yaryar, Mogadishu, 1965;] and also various publications in the magazines *Iftiinka Aqoonta* (1966, N1-6) and *Horseedka*.

[3] 'Faaliyihii la bilkeyday', – *Galaal, Andrzejewski*: 49-61.

[4] The poems were composed by Muuse Galaal; see *Galaal, Andrzejewski*: v.

speaks to him, they exchange an oath of friendship and the snake tells him (in verse) the desired prediction in exchange for his promise a share of the reward. The soothsayer goes to the sultan and passes on the prediction: a year of enmity is coming. The tribe gets ready for war in good time and comes out the victor. The sultan rewards the soothsayer with livestock; instead of giving the serpent his share he tries to kill him, but the serpent escapes.

The next year, the chief demands another prediction. The soothsayer appeals to the serpent, who forgives him and predicts a drought. The soothsayer goes to the sultan, the tribe gets ready for the drought in good time and manages to survive. The sultan rewards the soothsayer again but once again he avoids repaying the serpent. The sultan wants to know what will happen for the third time. The soothsayer goes to the serpent and returns with the prediction of rain. The tribe has time to prepare the reservoirs for water and avails itself of the generosity of nature in full measure. Everybody is replete and happy.

This time the soothsayer drives all the livestock with which he was rewarded to the serpent, begs forgiveness for the past and, acknowledging the serpent's higher wisdom, asks to be told about the structure of the world and the life in it. The serpent refuses the gift and the friendship of the soothsayer and says: 'World there is, but life is not distinct from it. Your life, as you call it, goes as the world goes, for God made the world with many patterns and it is these that rule men's lives. When war is the pattern of the times all men are at enmity with each other, and thus it was that during wartime you took your sword against me even after I had helped you, and said to yourself, "Cut off his head!" And then again, at a time of drought no man is generous to his fellows, so you ran away with all your herds, giving me no share in the sultan's reward. But when there is a pattern of prosperity… then you come to me, offering me all you have, not keeping even one animal for yourself. Each time it was the pattern, not yourself, that forced you to do whatever you did.'

What is the immediate impact of the tale? The closure comes, of course, with the final monologue of the serpent, who formulates the innermost meaning of the tale, elucidating in retrospect the manifold peripeties of the plot. This new understanding is unexpected but also well prepared, causing the listener/reader to experience a powerful shock of recognition – a sudden grip on the meaning of life as it appears in the tale. One is literally on the verge of exclaiming: 'Aha! That's it! So true!'. How is such an effect achieved? To answer this question, we must demonstrate, for the course of the tale as a whole and for each one of its episodes, the way they work for its central conceit, bringing it home on the crest of an aesthetic experience caused by the narrative. In other words, we must identify the function of every component in successfully realizing the theme.

This calls for a 'generative' description, specifying the text's derivation from its theme in accordance with the principles of artistic expression[5]. This project is an updated version of a traditional literary-critical problem: an attempt to reconstruct, in a painstakingly explicit and graphic step-by-step manner, the creative logic inherent in works of literary art.

2. The theme

The literary scholar usually begins by groping intuitively for the formulation of the text's theme. In our case, this is made easier by the serpent's final words: *life echoes the structure of the world,* i.e., people's actions are not free but determined by fate. This sounds close to the myth of Oedipus[6], except that our tale does not involve two conflicting concepts of causality (fatal inevitability *vs.* freedom of will). The serpent states that life *echoes* the structure of the world, not that it is *determined* by it; indeed, the actions of the soothsayer are *connected* with the general course of events in the sense that they

---

[5] See *A.Zholkovsky,* La poetica generativa di Eisnstein, in Cinema e Film, 1967, 3; *A.K.Zholkovskii, Yu.K.Shcheglov,* Strukturnaia poetika – porozhdayushchaia poetika, in: Voprosy literatury, 1967, 1 (English version: Structural poetics is generative poetics, in: Ed. by *D. Lucid,* Soviet Semiotics, Baltimore & London: Johns Hopkins University Press, 1978).

[6] i.e. the myth's explicit meaning and not those archetypal oppositions reconstructed by scholars (see *Claude Levi-Strauss,* Anthropologie structurale, Paris, 1958). Remarkably, in Sophocles' 'Oedipus Rex,' fate triumphs in the plot (borrowed from the myth) but the protagonist (Oedipus) proves equal to fate. Sophocles achieves this by structuring the tragedy as an investigation conducted by the suspect himself, resulting in his sentencing himself to a punishment carried out by himself.

are *similar to* it, rather than that they are *caused by* it. Never does the tale suggest that the soothsayer attacked the serpent *because of* fighting in battles; or that he kept the livestock *because of* the drought and general scarcity; or that he felt like giving *because* he had enough himself and saw generosity all around him. Only in the denouement do we find out that there has always been a connection within each of the three pairs of events, but that it is *not a causal connection* in the chain of causes and effects but a simple *similarity*, based not on the impact of one phenomenon upon another, but on a certain hidden affinity between the phenomena[7]. This view is presented in the tale not as merely a correct idea or even a striking truth, but as the most absolute of all truths: *a revelation*. The theme of the tale thus is:

A revelation: people's life is not independent; it is connected with the structure of the world by a relation that is not causal, but rather one of permanent mystical affinity. In short, revelation: life resembles the structure of the world.

3. Emplotting the theme

Outlining the overall composition of the "future" work can be envisaged as relying on random devices, but they would have greater explanatory power if their choice were determined by the theme. The scholarly legacy of Sergei Eisenstein abounds in instructive examples of detecting the devices that are inherent in the themes they are applied to. Following in his footsteps, let us try to identify devices cognate to our theme, *revelation: life resembles the structure of the world,* by examining its major components: (i) *resemblance;* (ii) *universality of the revealed law;* (iii) *revelation.*

(i) The idea of *resemblance* naturally predisposes the use of similes and comparisons. The static (eternal, universal) nature of these resemblances and the emphasis on affinities (rather than causality) also favor metaphorical patterning.

---

[7] This is similar to Leibnitz's 'monadic' view of the world, according to which every entity, or *monad*, is designed like a clock: it reflects the Universe not because the Universe (through other monads) affects it, but because there is a pre-established harmony between the changes in all the monads, creating a false impression of an interaction.

(ii) *Laws* (of life and nature) are best conveyed through multiple examples illustrating their universality[8]. Both the general rhetorical rule of diversifying the material and the specific task of rendering the laws' universality prompt the use of the expressive device of maximal, even contrastive, variation.

(iii) *Revelation*, i.e. a profound truth, first concealed from the people and then suddenly, often divinely, made known to them, involves the motif *recognition*, or epiphany, which is usually engineered by a narrative reversal, a sudden turn to the opposite course of events, imbuing the plot with suspense.

Collating the products of the three devices will yield the following outline of the emerging narrative:

a plot with a sudden turn towards the revelation of the multiple metaphorical correspondences proving that life is similar to the structure of the world.

This compositional sketch poses further generative tasks. In order to deploy the device of sudden turn, it is necessary first to formulate the anti-theme, i e. the opposite of the theme, that will provide the initial (pre-reversal) stage of the plot, and find means for concretizing it. It is also necessary to resolve the contradiction between the static nature of the theme proper and the dynamism of its narrative development.

Let us begin by formulating a statement that is opposite to the serpent's revelation ('World there is, but life is not distinct from it. This so-called life echoes the structure of the world'). It will look something like: 'Life as such exists, but there is no structure to the

---

[8] "How does this thesis [the implacability of time in a text by Ovid]... turn into an artistic image and obtain persuasiveness and strength? '1. A bull gets used to a yoke, a horse to a bridle, a lion loses its rage, an elephant starts to obey its master... 2. Fruits become sweet, grapes fill with juice, granules ripen in an ear of corn... 3. A tooth of a plough, a stone, a diamond, is ground down... 4. Anger and grief abate'. Objects are taken from all possible spheres of reality... so that they supplement each other, presenting together a... complete picture of the world, while the subjects... display different and sometimes opposite qualities... and are evenly scattered within each appropriate sphere." (*Yu. Shcheglov*, K nekotorym tekstam Ovidiya, in: Trudy po znakovym sistemam, 3, Tartu, 1967: 173-174.)

world'. In composing the tale we will have first to produce the picture of *life as such that is separate, formless, meaningless, not connected to the structure of the world.*

Another relevant aspect of the theme proper is the *static* nature of the world and life in it, one based on *affinities* among phenomena. The anti-theme should then paint the picture of a *dynamic*, narratively suspenseful beginning of the plot, foregrounding characters' *interactions* and other *cause-and-effect relations*. Since causality is only an illusive appearance, the dynamic interactions must be presented as occasional, ephemeral, incoherent ones. But in order to ensure the eventual readability of the revelation, the portrayal of *meaningless life* should be covertly infused with manifestations of the universal law.

These decisions result in a plot based on contrasting, and then combining, the anti-theme: *a formless, patternless life, with its ephemeral temporary dynamic interactions*, with the theme proper: *eternal static laws representing the metaphorical structure of the world.*

The contradiction between the static law of affinity and the dynamism of the plot has thus appeared in a new light: as a sought-out rhetorical contrast, one not to be eliminated or smoothed out, but rather emphasized, so as to allow a spectacular fusion of its opposite poles in a single plot line. The plot will proceed under the predominance of the anti-theme until a sudden triumph of the theme proper – a switch from a plot narrative to a meditative mode, a turn not *in the plot* but *from the plot to a non-plot*, to a 'non-narrational, lyrical, metaphorical, poetic' view of the world. It is worth noting that this way of matching the components of the overall theme with their respective means of expression (theme proper '! *poetic similes*, anti-theme '! *plot interactions)* is a remarkable peculiarity of our tale: its, as it were, valuable 'artistic discovery'[9]. Thus, we obtain a blueprint of

a plot with a sudden turn from a story of life as such, with its occasional temporary interactions, towards the poetic revelation of the static proportions between life and the structure of the world, developed with repetitions and contrastive variations.

---

[9] About the notion of 'artistic discovery' see: *L.A.Mazel*, Estetika i analiz', – 'Sovetskaya muzyka', 1966, 12: 20-21.

4. Detailing the plot

Next, the plot outline must be developed into concrete situations and interrelations among characters.

The proportion *life resembles the structure of the world* can be concretized as follows: *manifestations of life, for example, people's actions, resemble the manifestations of the world, for example, the divine phenomena.* With a threefold folkloric repetition this will yield: *action 1 resembles phenomenon 1, action 2 resembles phenomenon 2, action 3 resembles phenomenon 3.*

The device of contrastive variation will have to be applied now both to the divine *phenomena* and the human *actions*. For the *phenomena*, it can result in, among other possibilities, the set obtaining in our tale. Indeed, *divine phenomena 1, 2, 3* are represented by *war, drought, rain.* The first is opposed to the other two as social is to natural; inside the natural elements, the opposition is even clearer: *rain* is opposed to *drought* as wet is to dry, abundant to scant, generous to stingy, life to death; while *war* and *drought* together are opposed to *rain* as disastrous is to beneficial. As a result the three phenomena supplement each other and, in a sense, cover the world as a whole.

As for the contrastive variation of *actions*, the tale has *sword stroke, reneging on a debt, repaying with a surplus.* The first two actions are opposed to the third as violations of a contract are to honoring it, while the first is opposed to the third as active (*aggression, generosity*) is to evasive (*stinginess*). All three actions form an even transition from actively bad to actively good behavior, as if spanning the entire range of possible actions.

To schematize the way such sets are created:

(1) For each member of the proportion (*actions/phenomena*) many possible illustrations are chosen: *actions* '! *attacking, defending, stealing, showing stinginess, giving, falling in love, betraying...; phenomena* '! *war, harvest, earthquake, flood, rain...*

(2) These illustrations are diversified: *actions* '! good (*defending, giving*) as opposed to bad (*attacking, stealing, betraying*); active (*attacking, stealing*) vs. passive (*being stingy, betraying*); violent (*attacking, defending*) vs. non-violent (*stealing, betraying, falling in love*) and so

forth; *phenomena '!* natural *(drought, flood, rain)* vs. social *(war, harvest, festivities);* top *(rain, eclipse, eruption)* vs. bottom *(earthquake, harvest);* earth *(harvest, earthquake)* vs. water *(rain, flood);* mountains *(eruption)* vs. sky *(eclipse, rain);* good *(harvest, rain)* vs. bad *(earthquake, eruption)* and so on.

(3) From among the diverse *actions* and *phenomena* that have a common dimension, e.g. being good, positive, beneficial *(rain, giving, defending…)* vs. bad, negative, harmful *(attacking, being stingy, betraying, earthquake…),* it is necessary to pick out those that differ maximally in other respects as well.

Each of the *phenomena (war, drought, rain)* appears in the plot not once but twice: first as prediction, then as fact. The undesirable monotony of these repetitions is avoided thanks to the semantic opposition itself (mental *vs.* real) and the additional stylistic contrast between verse (rendering the predictions) *vs.* prose (narrating the events). The opposition is further dramatized by narrative suspense (Will the prediction come true? Will he share the reward?).

Such are the major moves in the multi-step process of creating the comparisons, repetitions and contrasts that convey the theme proper of *resemblance.*

As for the anti-theme, it is to be concretized through a plot sequence, i.e. something along the lines of *the protagonist first acting wrongly, but eventually going right,* except that, in order for this course of events to look 'meaningless,' the change for the better should be deprived of its causal, teleological sense, for instance, the way it is done in the tale: the serpent ignores the misdeeds of the soothsayer and readily agrees to help him again and again and at the end declines what seemed to be the deserved and long-awaited gift[10].

One of the requirements of the 'sudden turn' construction is combining the main manifestations of the theme proper with those

---

[10] The effect of 'meaninglessness' also has a narrative function: by making the reader feel dissatisfied with the narration it suggests the existence of a hidden meaning. The problem will be resolved in the ending, when the illusiveness of plot connections, especially from the point of view of the serpent, becomes clear.

of the anti-theme into a single chain of events. This means that the two sets of manifestations, so far connected only by resemblance, should now be bound by contiguity, that is, form a plot sequence of the protagonist's actions in the midst of the world's phenomena.

Let us combine *aggression* and *stinginess* with *the wrong actions* of the character, and *generosity* with *correct ones,* i.e. let him *display aggression and stinginess when in the wrong, and generosity after mending his ways,* and do so *in time of war, drought and rain respectively.* Let us also combine the *revelation* with the *event providing the sudden turn,* thus making the *revelation* the *denouement* of the plot.

At this juncture, we obtain

a plot that from the history of the character who in connection with war and drought does wrong (attacks, displays stinginess) but later, reforming himself, displays generosity in connection with rain, turns to the revelation of what is really important: that all the human manifestations (aggressiveness, greed, generosity) are similar to the divine ones (war, drought, rain).

5. Engineering the reversal

To make the shift to the *revelation* both unexpected and well prepared, the unfolding plot must, on the one hand, contain the material and even the pattern of the future revelation but at the same time keep it hidden from the reader. If in the end it turns out that *actions 1, 2, 3 resembled phenomena 1, 2, 3 respectively,* then in the course of narrating the plot they must appear quite *dissimilar.* Once again, deploying maximal variation is in order, but in a new way now. So far it has been used overtly, letting the reader notice from the start and enjoy the similarity in difference (*war, drought, rain* are *different* as such but *similar* as *world phenomena;* the same goes for the protagonist's actions). Now the difference between similar entities will have to be pushed to such an extreme that their similarity will become unrecognizable, making eventual recognition all the more startling.

The initial opposition *life vs. world* has yielded the antithesis *actions of one person vs. phenomena affecting the fate of people and nature.* This makes the two opposites quite different, but not different enough.

Creating unrecognizability is basically a compositional task and calls for compositional means: the dissimilarity of the opposites can be achieved by their maximum separation in the tale's narrative space. One way of making them non-comparable is splitting the plot into two stories, one internal, or framed, the other external, or framing, to be suddenly fused in the denouement. The inequality of their narrative status will hamper their comparison and make them incommensurable[11].

To split the plot into a framing story and a framed one, narratives resort to *message* motifs (*songs, recollections, dreams, orders, letters, etc.*). Our sketch already contains something of the sort: a *revelation*, which, along with such motifs as *presentiment, prediction* and others, is, indeed, a type of *message*. Bringing the plot's *protagonist* in line with the motifs of *revelation* and *prediction* and the cosmic scale of the theme will, in turn, prompt the raising of the social rank of the characters (yielding *divine creatures, kings* and whole *nations*) and result in the figure of *the provider of magic predictions*. The sequence of *the actions of the predictor* will naturally form *the framing story; the divine phenomena (war, drought* and *rain*), i.e. *the objects of the predictions,* will constitute the *framed story.*

The *actions of the protagonist* (the framing story) must be connected, plotwise, with the *events* of the framed story, while at the same time being far removed from it – in time, place and motivation. With this in mind and in tune with the elements *generosity/stinginess* and *right/ wrong,* we can cull from the traditional folktale repertoire the motifs of *contract, king's order,* and *reward*; coordinating this with *prediction* will result in *a prediction stipulated by a contract, an order* and *a reward.*

---

[11] Compare the plot of the Babylonian 'Dialogue of the Master and the Slave about the Meaning of Life,' which consists of ten episodes; in each, the master orders the slave to make certain preparations (to go to the court, to help a friend, etc.), then listens to his speculations about the futility of these intentions and cancels his order. In the last episode, the master, who is now convinced of the futility of life, decides to die and gives the corresponding order, stipulating, among other things, the burying of the slave together with his master. Thus the slave, who at first acted only as a discussant and executor of the orders, becomes the object of the last and most fatal one.

As a next step, *the provider of predictions* can be split into *an oracle* and *a soothsayer*, who will provide the characters of the framing story. *Contract, order,* and *reward* will play the role of additional links, augmenting the length and flexibility of the plot chain and driving its ends *(actions* and *phenomena)* even farther apart. As a result, the compositional separation (into two stories) can be supplemented by a separation in the plot (of the two characters), a temporal one (they will communicate *before and after* the war, i.e. during a time of peace, *before and after* the drought, etc.), and a spatial one (their meetings will take place outside the main scene of action).

These new narrative moves will help foreground the motif of *revelation.* The resemblance of the soothsayer's actions to world events will pass unnoticed through the end, creating a narrative need for an explicit announcement. Once stated, the resemblance will be perceived not as a moral tacked on to the tale, but as the denouement of the plot, i.e. as a long-awaited and necessary revelation clarifying the structure of the story and the world[12].

The introduction of the motifs of *contract, order,* and *reward* will also further develop the motif of 'meaningless life as such' by engaging the reader's attention with the superficial, causal aspects of *actions* and *phenomena,* i.e. questions like: Will the soothsayer manage to make the prediction? Will he honor the contract? Will he be punished by the serpent? Will they make peace in the end? and so on. Although the tale concerns the fortunes of an entire people and Fate itself is involved in them ('I am… Fate,' says the serpent), most of the time the plot focuses on the everyday needs of an average man: his

---

[12] The combination of a wise remark with a denouement ending in a punch line is a widespread device in Somali tales, e. g.:
Once a man gave shelter to a boy but did not feed him. At night a hyena came, took the boy and carried him away. The greedy man caught up with the hyena, snatched the boy away and said to him, ' True, I didn't give you food last night, but now I did save you from the hyena. Do I deserve your gratitude?' 'No, you do not,' the boy said. 'You don't like it when something falls into someone else's mouth – you just wanted to keep the hyena hungry!'
The plot resembles our tale in that the apparent change in the man's behavior (from bad to good) also exhibits the preservation of the status quo (denying food, this time to the hyena), as captured by the punchline.

attempts to avoid punishment, do his job, get a reward, and handle his debts.

An even more ambitious task is to project the tale's anti-theme, i.e. the *meaninglessness and transitoriness of life*, onto the storyline of the *divine oracle*. To do so, let us turn the *oracle* into a character of the framing story and link him with *the soothsayer* by *materialistic property relations* – via the motifs of *contract* and *reward*. Let us also make *the oracle's predictions*, important and correct as they are, into *separate predictions valid for one year only and pertinent to only one (internal) storyline*, and what's more, limit them to forecasting *specific events*, rather than intimating *ultimate eternal truths about the world as a whole*. Finally, let us use the problematic character of predictions to heighten the suspense (Will they come true?), further widening the gap between the *oracle's predictions* and his final *revelation*.

At this still intermediate but fairly advanced stage we can stop our simulated generation of the tale's plot:

Motivated by an order and the promise of a reward, a soothsayer concludes a contract with an oracle about prediction; they communicate in a special place and at a special time. As predicted, war, drought and rain one after another occur. The soothsayer is rewarded each time but acts respectively aggressively, stingily and generously towards the oracle. In the end, the oracle reveals to him that the actions of people, including those of the soothsayer's, have an affinity with the course of world events: life resembles the structure of the world.

MUSE - A WONDERFUL PERSON

Sheila Andrejewiski

I first met Musa in February 1950 in Sheikh, where he was a teacher at the famous School there. My husband, whom some of the older readers will remember as Goosh, had been looking for a job after university when the contract to work in Somaliland was offered to him by the Colonial Development and Welfare Department of the Colonial Office in London. For this he was required to learn Somali and to produce a scheme to write an alphabet for it. He leapt at the chance, though at the time we had no idea how life-changing this opportunity would be.

Goosh was very lucky that Musa was chosen by the Director of Education, Chris Bell, to be his assistant. The actual work involved in discovering the structure of Somali grammar was quite boring for them both; it meant hours of repetitive reciting of variations of sentences like "Did Ali meet Hassan? - Ali did not meet Hassan - Ali met Hassan" which Musa had to record on old-fashioned acetate discs. (Incidentally, these discs are stored in the Recorded Sound department of the British Library in London). But Musa soon found his own way of making these sessions more interesting for them both; he would quote a line of poetry, or a proverb, which contained the particular grammatical form which was needed, instead of the boring formulas about Ali and Hassan. I remember the delight with which Goosh told me he had found a fellow-poet to work with; he himself was a poet in his native language, Polish.

Musa was far too impatient to be able to actually teach Goosh how to speak Somali. Like many people who love their native language, he could not bear to hear it being mangled in the mouths of foreigners, and even many years later when Goosh was quite proficient in Somali, Musa could remark quite sharply that he used a particular expression too much. Goosh found that instead, our night watchman was very willing to tell him simple children's stories for hours on end, and gradually he began to understand the language.

Musa was extremely kind to me in my struggles with my new domestic life. He understood my wish to do my own cooking and soon found me a very pleasant middle-aged man who would help me only with shopping and cleaning. Musa was always willing to listen to me, and ready with a solution to any problem I might have.

But above all he seemed to know everything about Somali life and culture, and we would all sit for hours with our tea and my home-made biscuits, talking and above all listening and learning. Everything I know about Somali life as it used to be, I learned in those sessions. Once I witnessed an illustration of these old ways: I saw a young man, followed by an equally young girl, approach Musa – they had eloped and had reached his uncle without being caught by her family. Musa arranged for them to be married, after giving the girl a lecture about the duties of a wife!

When we returned to London Goosh was employed as a lecturer at the School of Oriental and African Studies and arranged for Musa to come to London to assist him in the same way as in Sheikh. This gave Musa opportunities for study , and he gained qualifications in linguistics as well as enjoying himself and making many friends here. He was as usual always full of jokes, often telling stories about foolish things he did (like queuing in a line of women in a hospital and being told it was for a pregnancy test). He was a wonderful person and I still miss him.

THE RIPPLE EFFECT: MUSA GALAL'S GIFT

Anita S Adam

Musa Galal's[1] contribution to documenting culture is well remembered and acknowledged by international Somali scholars, and his published work on folklore, poetry, and stellar and weather lore in the pastoral tradition can be cited in this regard. In addition, of course, in his everyday life, in the variety of roles of friend, of teacher, or through discussion and recitations at *qat* sessions akin to literary soirées, his cultural authority found further expression. The full extent of his influence however may be impossible to quantify, in that the hundreds of people who would have come under his spell in his lifetime will, like me, have their own memories of him as a peddler of folklore, and promoter and analyst of a people's literary heritage.

It is now thirty years since Musa died, and it is fitting that in conjunction with this anniversary, Kayd Somali Arts and Culture (KSAC) and Redsea Online Cultural Foundation have chosen to mark the launch of their new literature initiative with a tribute to Musa. KSAC's planned literature exchange project, says director Ayan Mahamoud, will engage in translating Somali literature into English and English works into Somali. The coincidence is fitting, not only because Musa Galal was a key figure in promoting Somali literature, he was one of the first to translate Somali works into English and make aspects of the Somali oral literary heritage accessible to Western scholars as well as to a range of other interested readers.

Elsewhere in this collection of narratives in memory of Musa is the very warm and affectionate personal reminiscence of Sheila

---

[1] Muuse Galaal (*Som.*).

Andrzejewski. My memories, whilst also drawing on personal knowledge, going not quite so far back as Sheila's, contain more tangential material, and allude to the extraordinary ripple effect that Musa's love and passion for his culture has had on others and on the protection and elevation of the Somali oral literary tradition in all its genres.

I first encountered the name Musa H. I. Galal in late 1963 whilst I was preparing to go and live in Somalia, and was reading whatever I could find on its history and people. Someone gave me a slim booklet called *A Somali Poetic Combat*. It was a bilingual Somali-English publication containing three poems in the classic oral poetic genre of *gabey*. They were by 'Ali Dhuh, Salan 'Arabi and Gaman Bulhan[2], and had been transcribed by Musa, using what was then an unofficial orthography for the Somali language, and translated into English in collaboration with a young B W. "Goosh" Andrzejewski – who would himself become renowned for his analysis and dissemination of Somali poetry and prose, and especially for his contribution towards a written Somali. The poems were about tribal conflict - part of a larger collection of what are known as *Guba* poems - and are as well known among Somalis as a Shakespearean play or sonnet among the English. *A Somali Poetic Combat* was memorable to me for being the only publication I came across at that time, half a century ago, which had a Somali name on its title page.

I carried *A Somali Poetic Combat* with me to Somalia in April of the following year. I vividly remember, two or three days after my arrival in Mogadishu, being introduced to the great man himself in the lift of the Shabelle Hotel. My husband and I were on the way to our room, and Musa was on his way up to the roof terrace which, in those halcyon Somali days, was a meeting place for poets and politicians, '*aqils* up from the provinces, and local worthies. Ever the raconteur, he could regale and charm any gathering, and no doubt he was as eager to get to his audience that early evening as they were to be entertained by his story-telling. I remember him then as a tall thin man, wearing Western dress and an embroidered

---

[2] Cali Dhuux, Salaan Carrabey, Qamaan Bulxan.

white *kofi*. The long slender fingers that stretched out to shake hands as we were introduced, felt that they could snap if grasped too hard. His trademark voice, piping and high-pitched, which one would learn to know well and which others I'm sure will remember, filled the small space as he spoke animatedly to the other people in the lift.

It was not long thereafter that Musa's little book was the instrument by which I came to realise the elevated status that poetic composition and oratory occupied in Somali culture, and that the enjoyment of poetry was not exclusive to an educated elite. In August Issa came down from Balidhiig to visit us. My brother-in-law was a nomad, and had never been to school. Relaxing on the verandah one evening, and with no common language of communication between us, I showed *A Somali Poetic Combat* to him, and began reading from the Somali script. After not more than two lines of this, Issa joined in the reciting of the poem, and we continued thus for a while, with me haltingly reading the Somali phonetic rendition and Issa reciting from memory, line by line, until he left me behind and went rhythmically on to the end. In recalling this incident, a comparison that seemed to me at the time apposite, and still today resonates, is the parallel with what we can gather about the Elizabethan 'golden age' of English literature when Shakespeare, Ben Johnson, Marlowe and their contemporaries were producing some of the most important works in English literature. As in the Somali case, their audiences were extremely diverse in terms of their social standing and education, and their works had likewise once enjoyed mass appeal. (Granted that they are still known and enjoyed today, but to rather more elitist audiences.)

Musa was a kinsman of my husband, and anyone who knows how Somali society works will understand that that would inevitably present many opportunities over the years for us to become better acquainted. My memories of such occasions comprise both the hazy and the clear, but one enduring memory is of his visits to our house, often on Friday mornings before attending the weekly congregational prayers at a nearby central mosque, when he would entertain the children with his storytelling. In this connection, my children and myself in different ways owe him a personal gratitude.

From him the children heard recounted to them the great legends of Arawelo and Deg Dhere, the Myth of the Maydi Tree[3], didactic folktales and much more, that was their Somali cultural heritage, and that I, from another culture, was unable to transmit. Moreover, to hear them told by one of the greatest national story-tellers – what an inheritance that is! On these occasions he would act and sing; like all good storytellers, he knew how to draw in and engage his audience, pausing at critical junctures in his narrative to ask of his mesmerised young listeners: 'What would **you** have done?' 'What would **your** wish have been?' In touching on this side of Musa's personality, we are reminded that no audience was too small, too young, or too insignificant for him. His pride in his cultural heritage, and the dissemination of it was for him a constant imperative.

Sheila hints at his penchant for telling stories against himself, and one such which I remember was his recounting of a time when as a student in the UK his tutor had raised the subject of Darwin's theory on the origin of species. 'Well', Musa said he had told his tutor, 'you may be descended from an ape, but my ancestor is Sheikh Is-aaq.'

Musa was in his final illness when we went to visit him at his home in Hodan, and later in hospital. It was not long after that we heard he had died en route to Jeddah for medical treatment. In recognition of his status as a national treasure, the government of the day, to its credit and despite Muslim convention in such circumstances, was resolute in having his body returned to his native land, where he was accorded a state burial. The name of Musa Galal continues today to be associated with the recording and transmission of Somali literary traditions.

[Somali words: *'aqil* – wise, intelligent person, elder; *qat* – mild recreational drug; Guba – from *gub* to burn or scorch–in this context used figuratively as inciting inner rage; *kofi* – hat, cap]

---

[3] Incidentally, I retold this delightful story in a set of Somali Study Materials for Schools which I produced under the Haan Associates publishing label in 1992. I have never been quite sure whether Musa himself created this children's tale, but I have never come across any other version or any other Somali who knew of it.

TRANSLATED POETRY FROM SOMALI WEEK FESTIVAL 2011 VISITING ARTISTS

MY APPRECIATION AND LOVE FOR POETRY TRANSLATION

Sarah Maguire

I first discovered how Somalis are obsessed with poetry when, about twenty years ago, I made friends with a man called Osman who worked at the checkout of my local Tesco's. I usually try to avoid telling anyone what I do for a living because of the bemused and often embarrassed looks I receive when I say I'm a poet. Osman was different though. He greeted my confession with delight and he immediately told me that poetry was more important to his people than practically anything else. Of course, at the time, this came as a complete revelation to me because, although I knew more about non-European poetry than most British poets, I was totally ignorant of Somali culture. Osman kindly offered to lend me *An Anthology of Somali Poetry* (translated by BW Andrzejewski and Sheila Andrzejewski) and once I'd read it, I was hooked.

My next encounter with Somali poetry was reading some excellent translations by Martin Orwin in a volume of *Modern Poetry in Translation* called 'Mother Tongues' edited by Stephen Watts. Again, I was deeply impressed by the inventiveness and energy of these poems and I was determined to know more. Fortunately, I was offered a writer's residency at SOAS and, in 2001, I stuck my head round Martin's office door and told him that one of my main aims in life was to turn Somali poetry into a cult, something I've done my very best to live up to ever since.

The next stage in this story is my founding The Poetry Translation Centre, thanks to the generosity and support of the Arts Council, in 2004. The PTC arose out of my residency at SOAS and the unique poetry translation workshops I'd begun to hold there in which, among many other poets, we'd begun to translate the work of Maxamed Xaashi Dhamac Gaarriye.

The PTC is a small, independent organisation dedicated to translating contemporary poets from Africa, Asia and Latin America. I founded the PTC for two main reasons. The first is that poetry thrives on translation. One example: that quintessentially 'English' verse form, the sonnet, was first devised in Italy. And so, if Thomas Wyatt hadn't translated the Italian poet Petrarch's sonnets into English, Shakespeare would never have written his remarkable sonnet sequence, one of the crowing glories of poetry in English.

As a young poet I was lucky enough to grow up reading wonderful translations of Russian and Eastern European poetry — a product of the then Cold War — but I became very aware that few excellent translations of contemporary poetry from, say, Arabic or Persian — let alone Somali — were available in English; this absence meant that English-language poets were prevented from enlivening their work through integrating the discoveries of their contemporaries.

The second impulse behind setting up the PTC was a growing awareness of the significance of poetry to a huge number of recent immigrants to this country. I was the first writer the British Council sent to Palestine and Yemen and, as a result I gained a unique insight into the role of poetry in Arabic and Muslim societies. What better way, it occurred to me, to make connections with these communities than by translating their leading contemporary poets into English and then bringing them here for readings and events?

In 2005 the PTC held its first World Poets' Tour, inviting leading poets from Afghanistan, India, Indonesia, Mexico, Sudan and Somaliland to give readings across the UK. I was absolutely astonished at the reception Maxamed Xaashi Dhamac 'Gaarriye' received from the crowds of excited Somalis who attended his readings. None of us had ever seen a poet welcomed with such wild delight and, as a result, it was clear to me that liaising with the Somali community was going to be one of our key priorities.

As I promised Martin all those years ago, I wanted to turn Somali poetry into a cult!

Gaarriye returned to work with us again for our second, hugely successful, World Poets' Tour in 2008. He inspired a group of young Somali men in Liverpool who were beginning to write poetry and he mesmerised audiences, Somali and British alike. And now, thanks to the generosity of Somali Week, we are delighted that we'll have another chance to work with Gaarriye and strengthen our ties with him and his community.

We feel very honoured indeed to have been invited to participate in the events and celebrations of Somali Week, especially as this year's theme is translation. Our own experience has proved that non-Somalis are intrigued and enthralled by the excellent translations of Somali poetry we've produced over the years, thanks in no small part to Martin Orwin, Maxamed Xasan 'Alto' and the poet, W N Herbert, who together have done so much to introduce English-speaking audiences to the rich tradition of Somali poetry. We look forward to many years of a deepening relationship between The Poetry Translation Centre and the Somali community.

EYES BRIMMING WITH BEAUTY

Axmed Shiikh Jaamac

Translated by Sarah Maguire and Mohamed Xasan 'Alto'

Ballaadhane is the name of a spring
That flows into the small lake of Hawd
A place that's to be found to the west of Burco
A journey or two from Bancawl
From where you first travel east
Before turning your face to the west.

Barni is the name of a girl
The length of her time on earth
Is more than a decade —
Add seven more years
And a handful of months.

Beloved, she has beautiful ankles
Is graceful and charming.

After a peaceful night
Just before dawn
The sheep began to stir
Baaing to their lambs to wake them up.

Barni alone heard their calls
Because she woke with the dawn
Eager to be the first to say Allah's name
Before the sun had started to rise.

She pulled on her shift
That sits next to her skin
Then dressed in her *boqor*

ISHII QURUXDA KA DHEREGTEY

Axmed Shiikh Jaamac

Gu'gu waa Ballaadhane,
Meeshu waa ballida Hawd,
Burco meel galbeed ka ah,
Bancawl geeddi iyo laba,
Bogox looga sii kaco,
Bidixna loo janjeedhsado.

Barni weeye gabadhuna,
Ma badnoo da'deeduna,
Tobankii u buuxsamay,
Toddobadi ku biirtiyo,
Bilo raacay weeyaan,
Waa bilan tagoog dheer,
Bilicsanoo la jecelyahay.

Deegaanku bari xalay,
Billowgii horreetaba,
Idahaa baraarugay,
Una baaqay naylaha,
Barni way maqleysoo,
Waabberi bay toostoo,
Bisinkiyo baryo Alley,
Ku balleeysay subaxoo.

Baftadeedi xidhatoo,
Beerkey ku laashoo,
Ma laallaadin boqorkii,
Waxay hawl ku baahdaba,

Absorbed with her work
At the height of noon
Barni can be found
Down in the valley
This is the place where the frogs can be heard
Croaking and calling loudly to each other
Where birds tweet and chirrup all day
A place that is lush with plentiful rain.

Late in the morning the sheep and goats
Were splayed out on the grass
Completely exhausted from stuffing themselves
Cows were mooing contentedly
Horses stretched their legs
As they shook their manes and tails
Free of burrs and bristles.

The young camel herders arrive at a run
Flushed with youth and vigour
Their powerful thighs mean they can leap
As high as a lion pouncing on its prey
All around is good pasture and fresh green shoots
Baby camels sleep on soft grass
Using each other as pillows
The tufts on their humps
Swaying softly in the breeze
When the little ones bray
Their mothers come to kneel down next to them
They nuzzle them and stretch out their necks
Murmuring with a soothing sound
The male camels also stand guard
Scanning the distance
Relieved of their duties
All have gained in stature and weight
And grown big and strong
They roll together in the sand
And chew their food into cud
Transfixed by all these heavenly scenes
Barni felt she was brimming with beauty.

Haddan oo barqa ah dheer,
Barni waxay dhex joogtaa,
Bulshaweynta dooxada,
Halka rahu ka bu'ayoo,
Buuqa isku darayoo,
Shimbiruhu bulxamayaan,
Biyo muguca weeyaan,
Adhyii oo barqaday baa,
Berrimada is wada wadhay,
Oo dharag bastood la ah,
Lo'dii baa bannaaxiyi,
Fardo baydda togayaa,
Baarkiyo qanaantiyo,
Bulkiyo saynta wada ridi,
Barbaarta geela jirataa,
Bardooddiyeysa orodkoo,
Bowdyo muruqyo adag iyo,
Booddada libaaxa leh,
Baad jilicsan iyo doog,
Bar cuddoon nirgaha seexdoo,
Isbarkaday dhammaanoo,
Bulbusha kurusyada,
Neecowdu baalbaashoo,
Markay? 'buuc' yidhaahdaan,
Ramag baasha dhow iyo,
Barbarrada ka joogaa,
Baaca dheer tusaayoo,
Bogga uga dunuunuci,
Baarqabkuna ilaaliyo,
Bidhaan eegid uu yahay,
Gaadiidka baayiray,
Owraha baruurtiyo,
Baaxaddiyo laxaadka leh,
Oo boodh iyo gelgelin tegeyoo,
Ku baduugay raamsiga,
Barni daawashiyo qurux,
Way bogatay maantaas.

UGH! TELEVISION IS REVOLTING!

Axmed Shiikh Jaamac

Translated by Sarah Maguire and Maxamed Xasan 'Alto'

You belong in the grave like all your kin from the Djinn
False hope, you're used by the Devil to hide all his schemes
You're employed by the Devil to broadcast his word
You're the Devil's head honcho, his officer-in-chief
You're the era's calamity, a miser on the rampage,
A mind-robber sent here from a continent far away.

If someone is docile you possess him without bloodshed
With a scalpel you cut open the top of his head —
A careful incision so no one makes a fuss —
They're all oblivious to your instruments and straps
In fact they'd run up the noose by themselves
As you parachute into another victim's judgement
You now have been granted pride of place in the house
Everyone I know has welcomed you in
You've kidnapped my family who once fled danger by my side
When you've shown them all these details
I wonder how on earth they make sense of it all.

Destruction, fistfights, nation attacking nation,
Gunpowder exploding, screaming and shouting
Villages on fire — flames reaching up to the sky
Everything smashed, knocked sideways, buildings emptied,
The treasury robbed and the rich made bankrupt
Swag bags slung over horses, hooves pounding
Kicking up dust against clamour and songs
When you've shown them all these details,
I wonder how on earth they make sense of it all.

CAKU TV-GA!

Axmed Shiikh Jaamac

Qabri lagugu tuuryaye jinkaad, qolo wadaagtaane,
Qalad la igu siray oo ibleys, ii qarshaad tahaye,
Qalab uu isagu keensaday oo, qaybsho yaad tahaye,
Qabbaankiisa weyn iyo sarkaal, uu qortaad tahaye,
Qudurrada sabaankiyo ibtilo, qooqan baad tahaye,
Maan-qalato yaad tahay ka timid, qaarad naga dheere.

Qofkoo hebed ah yaad kala baxdaa, dhiig adaan qubine,
Qobka madaxa saabaan qabow, yaad ku qodataaye,
Dadku yaanay qoonsane sarmada, wow qunyareeysaaye,
Qabatooyinkaagiyo xadhkaha, kama qaloodaane,
Iyagaaba qoolkaad ku ridi, soo qalqaashada'e,
Qariib baad ahayd shalay ku dagay, qoobad iyo laabe.

Imminkana qor saayid ah adaa, qaytay gurigiiye,
Dadkaygii qaraabiyo xigtaba, wuu ku qaayibaye,
Iga qaadday qoyskii dhammaa, aan la soo qaxaye,
Qorshe aad sameeysiyo markaad, qaabab ugu keento,
Qisadaada waan yaabay siday, ugu qushuucaane.

Qacda iyo baftiyo weerarkiyo, qoomamka is-laayay,
Baaruudda qaraxeeda iyo, qayladiyo wiida,
Qaryadaha gubtee ololo iyo, qiiqa kor u duulay,
Qalfoofkiyo alaabada qalliban, daaradaha qaawan,
Qasnadaha la boobiyo haddeer, qaniga caydhoobay,
Qandiyada la saariyo fardaha, qoobka roganaaya,
Siigada u sii qayan cirkiyo, qawdhankiyo heesta,
Qorshe aad samaysiyo markaad, qaabab ugu keento,
Qisadaada waan yaabay siday, ugu qushuucaane.

Sunrise over the lush, green earth
Rivers that course to the sea
Forests growing tall sprouting fresh leaves
Orchids in bloom shivering in the breeze
Animals of prey circling each other
Qamar selling up shop stuffed with luxury items
The significance of love, declaration and confession
When you express its sweetness to the full
On Fridays the entire family won't need to eat
When you've shown them all these details,
I wonder how on earth they make sense of it all.
But if I try to protest I face a brick wall
You turn me into an ignorant, contentious old man
So come here and tell me what you want me to say!

Qorrax soo baxaysiyo dhulkoo, qurux leh oo doog ah,
Webiyada qulqulayee ku dara, qooriyada xeebta,
Kaymaha qummaati u baxee, qawlku ruxanaayo,
Ubaxyada qadhqadhayee ku yaal, qadowga baashiisa,
Ugaadh qaarba dhan u jeeda oo, kala qammaadaysa,
Qamar iibinaysiyo dukaan, qaali lagu teedshey,
Adduun qaayihiisiyo jacayl, laysu qiranaayo,
Marka aad qiyaas ugu shushubi, qooshka malabaysan,
Quraac iyo ayaamaha Jimcaha, qado ma doonaane,
Qorshe aad samaysiyo markaad, qaabab ugu keento,
Qisadaada waan yaabay siday, ugu qushuucaane.

Aniguna haddaan qawl hollado, waa qar soo dumaye,
Oday qaxar ah baad iga dhigtiyo, jaahil qaraweyne,
Heshiis igu qasab ah keenso oo, qodobbo ii yeedhi

YOU UNDERSTAND

Saado Cabdi Amarre

Translated by Sarah Maguire and Mohamed Xasan 'Alto'

Hooyaallayey hooyaallayey, hooyaallayey hooye;
Weapons' factories thud with a pounding rhythm
Armaments spewed out to all the corners of the globe
With no boundaries, no limits and with no restrictions
Even a camel-herder slings an AK-47 on his shoulder
You understand the extreme suffering this brings

Black people, white people, non-believers, Muslims
It's men who burn to annihilate the land
They set up rockets and won't listen to arguments
While women plead for caution under the tree of peace

They've exterminated camels, cattle, goats and sheep
Wild animals — even the shielded tortoise — have all been slaughtered
You understand how many people have been slain in open fields
How birds have fled the countryside and migrated far away
You understand how this is getting like Hiroshima
You understand the destitution this visits on the world

Black people, white people, non-believers, Muslims
It's men who burn to annihilate the land
They set up rockets and won't listen to arguments
While women plead for caution under the tree of peace

You understand war and the injury it inflicts
You understand how loved ones are struck down
You understand how children are made orphans
You understand how the elderly are slaughtered
You understand how the world straps on a gas mask

WAAD GARAN LAHAYDEENE

Saado Cabdi Amarre

Hooyaallayey hooyaallayey, hoyaallayey hooye;
Warshadaha madfaca gaw leh iyo, gumuca beeraaya
Hubkan dunida kala gooshayee, gees walba u raacay
Ee aan xuduud lagu gartiyo, gogol-dhac loo yeelin
Aakeyga kii geela jirey, saaran garabkiisa
Intuu halista gaadhsiiyay baad, garan lahaydeene.

Inta gibil madow, inta gibil cad, gaaliyo Islaamba
Rag uun baa arlada gubee, waan la garanayne
Iyagaa gantaallada rakibay, mana gar-qaataane,
Waa kuwaa haweenkii guddiyay, geedkii nabadeede.

Geeliyo lo'dii buu jaray iyo, gaabanow adhiye
Geyi aan ugaadhiyo ku hadhin, diin gangaamaniye
Intuu gegida meyd jiifiyaad, garan lahaydeene,
Shimbirihii geyiga joogay ayaa, guuray oo qaxaye
In Hiroshiima gaadhsiisanyaad, garan lahaydeene,
Dhibtuu dunida gaadhsiiyay baad, garan lahaydeene.

Inta gibil madow, inta gibil cad, gaaliyo Islaamba
Rag uun baa arlada gubee, waan la garanayne
Iyagaa gantaallada rakibay, mana gar qaataane,
Waa kuwaa haweenkii guddiyey, geedkii nabadeede.

Colaad iyo waxay geysataad, garan lahaydeene
Inay gacalka naafeeysataad, garan lahaydeene
Gurbood inay agoomaysataad, garan lahaydeene
Odayada inay gawracdaad, garan lahaydeene
Inay dunida gaas-maas sudhaad, garan lahaydeene

You understand how hatred and bitterness persist
You understand how blameless villages are torched
You understand the extreme suffering this brings

Black people, white people, non-believers, Muslims
It's men who burn to annihilate the land
They set up rockets and won't listen to arguments
While women plead for caution under the tree of peace

You understand peace is a broad-leafed tree
You understand peace shelters families and friends
You understand peace brings prosperity
You understand peace is a churn of frothing milk
You understand peace means marriage and love
You understand peace escorts the married couple home
You understand peace is a place where happiness springs
You understand peace promotes progress
You understand peace is a home with a strong fence
You understand peace spreads like silk
You understand peace is an independent female camel
You understand peace brings knowledge and education

Black people, white people, non-believers, Muslims
It's men who burn to annihilate the land
They set up rockets and won't listen to arguments
While women plead for caution under the tree of peace.

Godob iyo wax baas inay tahaad, garan lahaydeene
Guryo negi inay ololisaad, garan lahaydeene
Intay halis gaadhsiisay baad, garan lahaydeene.

Inta gibil madow, inta gibil cad, gaaliyo Islaamba
Rag uun baa arlada gubee, waan la garanayne
Iyagaa gantaallada rakibay, mana gar qaataane,
Waa kuwaa haweenkii guddiyey, geedkii nabadeede.

Inay nabadi tahay geed hadhlaad, garan lahaydeene
Inay gacal xannaanaysataad, garan lahaydeene
Geel dhalay inay daaran tahaad, garan lahaydeene
Inay gaawe xoor badan tahaad, garan lahaydeene
Geyaan iyo jacayl inay tahaad, garan lahaydeene
Gelbis iyo aroos inay tahaad, garan lahaydeene
Inay goob farxadi taal tahaad, garan lahaydeene
Inay horumar gaadhsiisan tahaad, garan lahaydeene
Inay tahay guryo deyrka laad, garan lahaydeene
Inay tahay xariir lagu goglaad, garan lahaydeene
Gobaad inay ku iidaaman tahaad, garan lahaydeene
Inay tahay aqoon loo gudbaad, garan lahaydeene.

Inta gibil madow, inta gibil cad, gaaliyo Islaamba
Rag uun baa arlada gubee, waan la garanayne
Iyagaa gantaallada rakibay, mana gar qaataane,
Waa kuwaa haweenkii guddiyey, geedkii nabadeede.

NEVER FORGET!

Saado Cabdi Amarre

Translated by Sarah Maguire and Mohamed Xasan 'Alto'

If you're elected as an impartial judge
But you tend to stick close to your clan
Corruption will be rooted in your mind
If you sell property behind the owner's back
You'll find yourself playing a dangerous game
Deception and fraud are the enemies of justice
There's a clear line between them
If you shun responsibility and turn your back on the law
If justice is muddied then confusion will reign.

Hey you, Xaashi! Look at the children robbed clean of everything
Look at the pleas of those women the judge ignored
An astonishing arrogance that now goes unnoticed
A nation of evil-doers will never progress
When lawyers themselves corrupt the law
When people are bribed and imprisoned for nothing
Wrong-doing in this life will be paid for after death
Peace is impossible unless evil is confronted

It's irrelevant that this man comes from my neighbourhood
It doesn't matter to the case if you are close to him
The trial doesn't concern any of these issues
Hey you, judge, focus on the facts and on justice
You've got blood on your hands, you're tainted with deception
You hide poison at the bottom of the bowl
Here justice is as pointless as a poorly-tied camel-halter
Because all the judges are so easily bought
Those who can't bribe are forced to walk through a thorn thicket

DHAB U XUSUUSNAADA!

Saado Cabdi Amarre

Haddii xubin garsoore sare iyo, xaqa laguu dhaarsho,
Xigto iyo qabiil iyo haddaad, xaynka ku asqowdo,
Laaluush xammuurani qalbiga, kaaga xididaysto,
Xoolaha qof leeyahay haddaad, mid u xalaaleyso,
Xammil-dhaafku awr wuu dilaa, xadhig qalloocdaaye,
Xumaatiyo inaan boolli iyo, xaqu walaaloobin,
Oo ay xad kala leeyihiin, waa xuruuf qorane,
Haddii aad xilkaagiyo bulshada, xeerarka u laabto,
Haddii uu xaqsoorku ambado, wareer kalaa xigi e.

Xaashiyow agoommada la dhacay, baaddilka iyo xoogga,
Dumarkaa xuquuqdooda maqane, xaakin uga dhaartay,
Xilliga iyo kibirkaa jiraa, cidi ma xaaleeyne,
Xumo uunka dadka wadaa, way xayiranyiine,
Xeer-beegtidoodaa kharribay, xaaladaa jira'e,
Xumaha shicibka loo geystey waa, xidh iyo laaluushe,
Xadkii dhaaftee aakhiro waad, xagal-ka-daacdeene,
Xumaatada haddaan layska qaban, ma xasilaysaane.

Kaasi xaafaddeennuu ahaa, maaha xaajaduye,
Kaasaad xidhiidh leedihiin, maaha xaajaduye,
Kaasina xigaal buu ahaa, maaha xaajaduye,
Xaashee garsooryahow ambaday, xaqa u soo laabo?!
Xinjir baad faraha kula jirtaan, sun iyo xaaraane,
Xeedhada gunteedaa dhunkaal, ku xafidaysaane,
Sida awr xidhiidh ku af-maddan buu, lumay xaqsoorkiiye,
Laaluush qofkii u xaddida bay, u xaglinayaane,
Xoolo iyo itaal kaan lahayn, xanan la jiidhsiiye,

My heart breaks at the suffering of so many people
It's an outrage if we can't bring justice into line
It's a disgrace if we don't all campaign for change.

If the judge breaks the law and says robbery's legal
If the judge makes friends with greed and wealth
Never forget the true judgement of the grave!
Never forget there's a grave with your name on it!
Never forget hell and its punishments!
Never forget heaven and its blessings!
Never forget Allah records all your deeds!
Never forget the Day of Judgement!
Never forget that God is Chief Justice!

Xaggooda iyo dhankooduu qalbigu, iga xanuunaaye,
Xumaha iyo haddaan baaddilkow, ku xakameeyn wayno,
Oon sacabka xeelad ugu tumo, waa xurmo-la'aane.

Xaakinkii bulshada dhaawacee, dhaca xalaaleeyey?;
Haddii xoolo geel iyo hunguri, kula xakaaloobo,
Xabaalo iyo qubuuraa jiree, dhab u xusuusnaada?!
Iil baa la kala xaadhayaa, dhab u xusuusnaada?!
Xuladdo iyo naar baa jiree, dhab u xusuusnaada?!
Xays bay jannadu leedahee, dhab u xusuusnaada?!
Ilaahay baa xisaabaha qoree, dhab u xusuusnaada?!
Xaadir aakhiraa imanayee, dhab u xusuusnaada?!
Xaakin buu Ilaahay ka yee, dhab u xusuusnaada?!

POLITICS

Jaamac Kadiye Cilmi

Translated by Sarah Maguire and Maxamed Xasan 'Alto'

First I spot nine colours
Next I read eight names
I hear thirty different speeches
With eighteen disparate views
And thirteen different faces
All poisoned by pessimism
Lacking focus and direction
Strangers one and all.

Is this really what's called politics?
It looks like a nest of vipers to me!
Politics unsettles everything
It turns the world upside down
It divides all the people
And foments great unrest
Everywhere it goes
It infects them with its poison.

Politics sneers at moral excellence
And thinks goodness is an irritant
It promotes evil deeds
And makes friends with deceit
Hiding behind the interests of the clan
While it takes a swindler along as a pal
It confides in deception
And flags up failure
In order to profit from what's going on.

Politics turns its back on the inspirational leader
It corrupts law and order

SIYAASAD

Jaamac Kadiye Cilmi

Sagaal midab baan arkaa,
Siddeed magac baa ku xiga,
Soddon hadal baan maqlaa,
Siddeed iyo toban af iyo,
Saddex iyo toban wajoo,
Saantoodu madowdahoo,
Sidaa u wareegayoo,
Silloon baan eegayay.

Waxaan ma siyaasad baa?
Subxaanyaa laga matalay,
Intaa way soconaysaa,
Sal iyo baar bay xushaa,
Dadkay kala soocaysaa,
Wax bay soofeeyneysaa,
Intaa salaggay martaba,
Sun bay ku afuufaysaa.

Wanaaggay saluugsantahay,
Samaantay ka dhiidhidaa,
Xumaantay saaciddaa,
Beentey saaxiib la tahay,
Qabiilkay la seexataa,
Sirrow bay weheshataa,
Sagsaaggay aammintaa,
Mid saaqiday bay tustaa,
Siduu u danaysan laa.

Saciimkay ka leexataa,
Waxay sarriftaa sharciga,

And spits out justice
Like a locust it gnaws at wisdom
And infects equal rights with its sickness
So that injustice can rule the roost
Politics greases the ladder
It is simply prejudice in action.

I tell you there are two sorts of politics —
But the Somali version
Is doomed from the outset

All the people who've been good
Just because they fear Satan
Politics strikes down with an evil spirit
This is the prize it is after —
When people line up on two sides
And set to attacking each other
When throat-slitting begins
When body and soul are sundered apart
Politics cheers from the sidelines
Shouting out 'keep up the good work'.

I tell you there are two sorts of politics —
But the Somali version
Is doomed from the outset

Politics kidnaps the innocent
It auctions off people's provisions
Swindling huge sums of cash
By impersonating the owners
Anything related to guns and machetes
Anything resembling weapons and ordnance
It purchases in bulk for the people
How on earth can we stop this from happening?
Believe me, that is the aim.

I tell you there are two sorts of politics —
But the Somali version
Is doomed from the outset
Politics is hostile to patience

Caddaaladday seegantahay,
Xaqsoorkay suus ku tahay,
Sinnaantay cudur ku tahay,
Dulmiga inuu sare maro,
Bay sallaanka u toosisaa,
Eex bay ka samaysan tahay.

Siyaasaddu waa labee,
Middeer Soomaaliyeed,
Sideedaba waa nuxuus.

Dadkii wada suubbanaa,
Ayuun bay sabab ibleys,
Mar qudha ku dhex sayrisaa,
Markuu dhiig wada sunsumo,
Iyadu subag buu u yahay,
Safayn goortay noqdaan,
Sarriib bay qaadataa,
Surgooyada laysu dhigo,
Naf iyo ruux la sugo,
'Sidiinnii u sii waday' dhahdaa,
'Saacaddii kastaba!'

Sedkooday qaadataa,
Saadkooday iibsataa,
Sawdkooday ku hadashaa,
Santuuqyay buuxsataa,
Wixii seefo iyo quryo ah,
Wixii sulub dhici lahaa,
Si fudud bay ugu gaddaa,
Sidee loo joojiyaa?
Ujeeddadu waa sidaa.

Siyaasaddu waa labee,
Middeer Soomaaliyeed,
Sideedaba waa nuxuus.

Qofkii samir iyo dulqaad,
Ku sugan bay colaadisaa,
Midkii salfudeedka neceb,

To people who are calm while they wait
To those who are always thoughtful
It hires contract killers
Employs bullying and force.

Politics sets traps
And lays down a noose
If someone slips free
Who loathes deception
Is untainted by evil
And immune to Satan's spells
That person should be safe and secure
Because 'crime never pays'.

I tell you there are two sorts of politics —
But the Somali version
Is doomed from the outset

Politics conjures up sorcery
It brings on fits and infections
It cooks up poison and wounds
It flourishes razor-sharp blades
Blades that can cut with a word
Politics nurtures the greedy
Who stockpiles goods for himself
It brings on alcoholism
And stunts children's growth
Politics is a lethal virus
Spreading sickness and crime
Politics is a wild beast
It provokes danger and terror
Terminal illness and pain
It sets relatives against each other
It tears families apart
And it marks the death of friendship

I tell you there are two sorts of politics —
But the Somali version
Is doomed from the outset

Saf bay u kireeysataa,
Inuu sandulle ugu kaco.

Silsilad bay daadisaa,
Siriq iyo dabin bay dhigtaa,
Haddii aanu surinka gelin,
Sagsaagga ka daacad yahay,
Xumaanta ka saafi yahay,
Ka saahido saar ibleys,
Midkaasaa samatabbaxa,
Sirroow, ma hodmaa la yidhi.

Siyaasaddu waa labee,
Middeer Soomaaliyeed,
Sideedaba waa nuxuus.

Fal iyo sixir bay dhashaa,
Sarciyo cudur bay dhashaa,
Sun iyo boog bay dhashaa,
Sakiimmo af lay dhashaa,
Mindiyo sarayay dhashaa,
Mid aan sedku deeqinoo,
Sibraarro watay dhashaa,
Sakhraan daran bay dhashaa,
Saqiirro xun bay dhashaa,
Sawaad durey ah bay dhashaa,
Saxar iyo dembi bay dhashaa,
Belaayo soke bay dhashaa,
Subaacyo shishey dhashaa,
Sas iyo halis bay dhashaa,
Dadkay sakaraadisaa,
Wax bay sinji doorisaa,
Wixii seeddi iyo abti ah,
Sokeeyaha wada dhashay,
Saaxiibkay kala dhishaa.

Siyaasad wixii yaqaan,
Caloosha wuxuu ku sido,
Haddii uu sari lahaa,

If we could disembowel
A so-called political 'expert'
If we could take him apart
And probe his insides
Anyone within reach
Would keel over unconscious
Anyone who comes within its orbit
Turns into a mealy-mouthed swindler
Someone who speaks solely in euphemisms
Who manipulates his erratic behaviour
Into a version of normality
Claiming his is the only perspective.

A politician can't give a straight answer
He won't listen to what you say
Before you can open your mouth
He comes out with something
That is utterly incredible
Like a madman
Teetering on the edge of a cliff
He fixes his eyes on the crowd
He projects multiple signals
By wildly flapping his hands
He conjures figures out of thin air
And weaves strange predictions
Based on anonymous data
What a travesty is displayed
What forgeries are created
What false statements are written
All those misguided people
Have been damaged by their politics
Which they think is normality

But one day sincerity will be rescued
Those who've escaped will be safe
Those who've waited will get their reward
And the deceiver will be destroyed
Because 'crime doesn't pay'.

Ama uu saafsaafi laa,
Wixii soonaha ka dhow,
Dadkuba wuu suuxi laa.

Wixii seeraheeda galaa,
Wax baa la saynsaabayaa,
Sarbeeb buu riixayaa,
Isagu sogordaha gurracan,
Wuxuu ku saleeynayaa,
Inay saxan tahay middan.

Su'aashuu diidayaa,
Isagoon hadalkaaga sugin,
Haddana laba sikin dhexdood,
Wuxuu soo celinayaa,
Mid aadan siddiqi karayn.

Sallaafi iyo waalli buu,
Qarhaysta u saaran yahay,
Si buu wax u eegayaa,
Seenyaaluu bixinayaa,
Gacmuhuu sayrsayrayaa,
Wax buu suuradinayaa,
Wuxuu saadaaliyaa,
Middii loo soo sajalay.

Maxay sawir muujisaa,
Saxiix maran qaadataa,
Qoraallo sameeysataa,
Waxaa ummad laysa sudhay,
Ayay sababtoodu tahay,
Haddana sahal moodayaan.

Daacadi way samatabbixi,
Sigtaa waa nabad galaa,
Samraa waa helaa sedkii,
Sagsaag waa khasaarayaa,
Sirrow ma hodmaa la yidhi.

THE SPEECH OF OUR LANGUAGE

Jaamac Kadiye Cilmi

Translated by Sarah Maguire and Mohamed Xasan 'Alto'

Utterance without weight
Spoken with no emphasis
And all frivolous speech
Is the death of our language

Our speech is our heritage
The most intricate poetry
A song to make us dance
And a song to help us work

It's *Heello* and *Buraanbur,*
It's chorus and refrain
Syllables and music
Conversation and veneration
Threats and boasts
Riddles and tales

Stories and facts
Our speech is our heritage
Spoken by our ancestors
It's the wealth of our people
Our children's treasure-house

It's the lodestone of our culture
Utterly indispensible
The means of seeking assistance

HAWRAARTA AFKEENNA

Jaamac Kadiye Cilmi

Hadalkii aan ujeeddiyo,
Himilo toosan lahayn,
Iyo hadaaq waa ku dilaa.

 Hawraari waa murtideenna,
Haddana waa gabaygeenna,
Ama heesta cayaarta,
Ama hawsha middeeda.

Heello iyo buraanbur,
Hooriskeeda iyo jiibka,
Higgaadda iyo luuqda,
Haasaawihiyo ammaanta,
Hanjabaaddiyo faanka,
Halxidhaaliyo sheeko.

Waa hiraab iyo toosin,
Waa afkii hiddaheenna,
Amase hooyo iyo aabbe,
Hantidii ummaddeenna,
Habistii ubadkeenna.

Waa hoggaan dhaqameedka,
Marna aan la hureyne,
Lagu soo hiranaayo.

HARMONY

Caasha Luul Maxamuud Yuusuf

Translated by Sarah Maguire and Mohamed Xasan 'Alto'

When the spring rains come the livestock give birth
Each lush new leaf stays plump
The fresh green grass is luscious and rich
Everyone gorges on water, drinking their fill
While the fresh rain falls evenly all around

With each step your footprints sink into the ground
And the soaked soil sucks at your heels
Birds sing their own songs all at once
And then the frog starts to join them

Brightly-patterned butterflies flit around new blossoms
Their beating wings like vivid flags flapping back and forth
As they drink in the aromatic breeze like water
Inviting everyone to come along and join them

Flowers seem to have been etched with henna
And they all spring upwards at once
After the heavy rain that fell the night before
Their ripe fruit glows deep red and nut-brown
Berries and fruit hang thickly from the shrubs
All tightly packed together
Many different fruits now ripen all at once
No throat they slip down would ever protest
No eyes that see them could complain
All this goodness can never be restrained

This magnificent sight
Is beyond human comprehension
It's beyond the power of human description

CUDDOON

Caasha Luul Maxamuud Yuusuf

Gugoo curtay cuudkii oo dhalayoo
Caleentii baxdoon carjabin weliyoo
Cagaarkiyo dooggu uu cusubyoo
Intuu cokan yahay biyii cabbayoo
Calcalyadu ceegaagto kadimmada.

Halkaad cagta saarto ciiraysoo
Rayskuna celinaayo cidhibtaadoo
Shimbiruu ciyayaan cod kala jaadoo
Cabbaar dabadeed rahuna u ceshoo.

Balambaallis cardhiinya lehoo cosobsatay
Celcelinaysa baalal calammo lehoo
Neecawda cabbaysa carafteedoo
Casuuntay intii la caynad ahayd.

Ubaxoo cutub-cutub cillaansamay
Curubta caaraddeedu simantahayoo
Caydhkii tumay cawadii hore oo
Hoobaantu casuus casaan yartahoo
Canbuushiyo midhuhu ciireenoo
Caashiyo isa saaray cidhifyadoo
Curdankii u bislaaday cayn-cayn,
Cunahay maraysana ka caagaynoo
Cuyuunkii arkaan cadhoonaynoo
Cindiga sanna caajis gelahayn.

Caynadday u egtahay cajiib badanaa
Caqliga aadamaan caddeeyn karinoo
Carrabka ruux ku sheegey baan curinoo

More fragrant than the most precious incense
I can only compare this perfume to sandalwood

In these four verses I tell of a perfect environment
Once my country was famous for its loveliness
Its soil is gold beyond price
A sanctuary, it's a place of peace and safety
Tonight I celebrate my country
And may it be healed by justice!

Under a clear sky with no hint of haze
Not a cloud to be seen, nor any mist
Not even the colours of a rainbow
Like the clarity of the first light after dawn
Or when the full moon hangs heavy in the sky

The best young people are chosen for the dance
Their songs and choruses echo harmoniously
While Cureeji and Caalin join in with delight
The skilful young men are alive with excitement
The graceful divas respond with their chorus
As the circle of dancers leaps with joy
When the climax comes the sun rises up
Bringing the party to a perfect end

The girls whose names are Canab and Cambaro
Have purified the churn with charcoal and clean cloths
Ready to be filled with milk for the children
Skilful mistresses of the churning of buttermilk
Their churns are full to the brim with ghee

All the people welcome each other with open arms
Families and villages live together in peace
People are generous and receive gifts with delight
There is no enmity, no one fears for their safety
Village elders and religious scholars are leading the way
So the community lives together in peace and fulfilment

In these four verses I tell of a perfect environment
Once my country was famous for its loveliness
Its soil is gold beyond price

Cadarkiyo ka udgoon cambarka la shitoo
Cuudkaan ku masaalay carafteedee.

Afartaa ku cabbiray cimilo wacanoo
Carrigaan u dhashaa ku caanbaxayoo
Ciiddiisaa dahaboon cid gooynaynoo
Caynaaniyo waa cawiyo nabadoo
Caawaba waanigaa ku ciidaayee,
Caddaalad ku caafimaad qaba!

Cirkoon caad iyo cirjiidho lahayn
Daruuri cudhanaynnin ceeryaan lihi
Jeegaan ku caweermin laba cayn lihi
Cadceed subax uun la caynad ahoo
Caddiyo dayax lagu caweysimoo.

Dhallintu isu cugteen ciyaartiiyoo
Cagtiyo jiibtu ay is celiyeenoo
Cureejiyo Caalin marayaanoo
Wiilashii carbisnaa cartamayaanoo
Cadrado luuqdii u celiyeenoo
Golihii cammirmoo cidhiidh yahay baa
Cakuye! Libdhadii caddaan noqotoo,
Ciyaartii ku dhammaatay caynkaa.

Hablihii Canab iyo Cambaro laa
Dhiilihii culaygiyo catiriyeenoo
Caanihii loogu shubay carruurtiiyoo
Ciirtii lulayaan cuddoon dumaroo
Codcodkuna ubbadii ku cigan yahay.

Calooshoo nadiif ah lays casumoo
Cashiiradu nabad ku wada ceeshtoo
Ciyigii laysa siiyey ceebli'iyoo
Colaad raagtiyo cabsiyi jirinoo
Cuqaal iyo culimmo talinaysoo
Caam ahaan cafis beeshu kala tahay.

Afartaa ku cabbiray cimilo wacanoo
Carrigaan u dhashaa ku caanbaxayoo
Ciiddiisaa dahaboon cid gooynaynoo

A true sanctuary, it's a place of peace and safety
Tonight I celebrate my country
And may it be healed by justice!

In the evening everyone walks home side by side
Bearing news from the neighbouring communities
Children spread palm leaves and prayer mats on the ground
A spacious place with neither discomfort or tension
Where people talk together honestly and openly
Where they have neither fears nor worries

The people are devout in their worship of Allah
They recite the Koran throughout the day
Allah has granted them honour and prestige
When I look at them I am full of admiration and love
May Allah never remove their prosperity and peace!

Caynaaniyo waa cawiyo nabadoo
Caawaba waanigaa ku ciidaayee,
Caddaalad ku caafimad qaba!

Carraabuu galabtii is ciirsadoo,
'Ceelkii ka warrama cidihii kale!'
Cawdiyo salligii ciyaalku dhigoo
Cidhiidhiyo aan cardoof jirinoo
Cafiif tahay sheeko caarif ahoo
Cabsiyo aan la qabin caloolyow.

Caabudaadda Alliyo cibaado gutoo
Cilmiga diinta iyo casharkii subciyoo
Cisiyo sharaf Caaddil ugu deeqyoo
Caynkaan u daydaba naftani calmatee,
Allow ha ka celin nimcadan u cammiran!

DISORIENTATION

Caasha Luul Mohamud Yusuf

The literal translation of this poem was made by Maxamed
Xasan 'Alto'. The final translated version of the poem is by
Clare Pollard

The boy that I love
was made handsome by God;
fine as a jewel.
My people, where is he?

I'm looking intently,
eyes fumbling -
confused -
conjuring him everywhere.
My people, where is he?

Whilst others sleep,
I'm sick with not-sleeping,
each faint, muddled voice
makes me strain to hear.

Nothing will nourish -
I don't eat or drink.
My throat's dry,
my lips crack,
a gag's in my mouth.

How many times has rain drenched me?
Drops pummel my skin,
then the storm's deep boom;
floods approach -
their ferocity sweeps me away like a stem.

How many times must I climb the mountain?
Wrestle through jungle,

JAHAWAREER

Caasha Luul Maxamuud Yuusuf

Wiilkaan jeclaayee,
Jamaal Eebbe siiyiyo,
Jawhara-la-moodkii,
Dhankuu iga jiraa, tolow?

Jeedaalo deydeyey,
Jalleecada indhuu tabe,
Jahawareerka igu dhacay,
Jaha kasta ka eegee,
Dhankuu iga jiraa, tolow?

Intuu jiifo aadmigu,
Hurdo wayga jarantahay,
Jabaqdii dhaqaaqdaba,
Waan juuq dhegeystaa.

Jalka iyo biyaha iyo,
Uma jeesto oontoo,
Waan jidiinqallalayoo,
Jaynafkaa dibnaha iyo,
Jiilku waygu go'an yahay.

Immisuu jir da'ay iyo,
Dhibic jawda haysiyo,
Jibin roobku tuuriyo,
Daad soo jaguugliyo,
Jirridda-gooye ila tegey.

Intaan jiidhey buuraa,
Ama jeexey kaymaa,

trek endless paths
or tumble down their steep slopes.
My soul doesn't stay stop,
it forces me on.
I heave myself onto the ledge for you.

How many times have the sticky trees,
the thorns, the acacia,
the bilcil's rough limbs
the shrubs, clingy weeds
the sog-sog dragged me away?

The venomous black snakes,
the pythons, coiled vipers,
the startled, slippery abeeso,
how many times have I stepped over them?
How many times must I outrun them?

I've wounded myself with love -
I've snapped bones, they leak marrow,
I'm flat on my back.
And this self-destruction, these difficulties
mean nothing, my dear.

Because of your love, Jamaal,
the male lion, maned,
creaking his fangs,
has caught a she-camel
and severed its artery.

With his jaw,
leaning forward,
he laps up the blood.
I keep near this creature.
It is my neighbour.
I'll stay here now, because of you.

The elephant with its tough hide
rears its trunk,
whips trees aside,

Waxa aan jid dheer maray,
Ama gebiyo ila jabay,
Joog ima tidhaahdee,
Naftu igu jujuubtoon,
Jar ka duulay awgaa.

Intaan jeerin qodax liyo,
Jiic iyo maraag iyo,
Bilcil jeenyo dheer iyo,
Jillabka iyo marabboob,
Sogsog jiitey awgaa.

Jilbiska iyo halaqiyo,
Jebis iyo mas duubnaa,
Jeefaaf abeeso leh,
Inta aan ku joogsaday,
Ee jiidhay badanaa.

Naf jacayl wareemoo,
Dhuuxa uu jejebiyoo,
Jeegada u taalloo,
Jamanaysa muuqaa,
Jabka iyo halaaggaa,
Uma jeedo, gacalow!
Jamaal, aawadaa baan,
Jooflaha libaaxoo,
Jiriqsanaaya micidoo,
Intuu Jaawo geel heley,
Kala jaray halbowlaa.

Isagoo jiriidkiyo,
Jeenyaha isdhafshoo,
Juruqsanaaya dhiiggaan,
Jabada kula negaado,
Jaahiisa u eegoo,
Ula jaaray awgaa.

Jiliflow maroodigu,
Markuu jiido gacankee,
Dhirta uu jibaaxee,

destroying the forest.
I don't mind this either.

I don't feel compassion.
I don't get gooseflesh.
Because of your love, Jamaal,
I stay with beasts now.
They are my neighbours.
I belong here, because of you.

All this hardship I endure,
all this wasteful pain,
it's because I love you.
My people, where is he?

Laamaha jejebiyana,
Naftu kama jidh-diiddoo,
Kama jixinjixootoo,
Jidhiidhico ma qabatoo,
Jamaal aawadaa baan,
Jabada kula negaadoo,
Jaahiisa u eegoo,
Ula jaaray awgaa.

Waxse aan jabkaas iyo,
Jirrabkaa u marayaa,
Jacaylkaaga weeyee,
Dhankuu iga jiraa, tolow!

PASSING CLOUD

Maxamed Xaashi Dhamac 'Gaarriye'

The literal translation of this poem was made by Martin Orwin and
Maxamed Xasan 'Alto'. The final translated version of the poem is by
David Harsent.

Setting sun
You're on the run:
Late afternoon
And gone so soon!
What are you scared of? What's the rush?
Is it the spears of light that shine
Back at you from rock and bush?
Is it the dark creeping up on you
Or bad news from the depths of night
That makes you want to hide your light?
Or is it this girl, more beautiful
Than rain in the season of drought, whose grace
Is greater by far than the subtle pace
Of a passing cloud when it's nudged by the wind?
When you and she exchanged glances just now,
It was you who grew pale, it was you who shrank
From the gleam in her eye and the glow of her smile.
Setting sun
You're on the run:
Late afternoon
And gone so soon!
Have you gone
To warn the moon
That she must face
This greater grace?
The roll of the clouds, the furl of the waves -
A sea of cloud stained purple and red,

FAD GALBEED

Maxamed Xaashi Dhamac 'Gaarriye'

Gabbal-dhaca cadceed-yahay
U sii faano-guratee
Casar gaaban liiqii
Godka weeraraysaa!
Go'e fuley miyaad tahay?
Waa maxay garmaamadu?

Ma googooska sagalkiyo
Gamasyada shucaacaa
Gaade kaa horreeyiyo
Gurigaad ku hoyan layd
War ku gubay ka soo direy?

Mise gabadhan dhoolkiyo
Gu'goo shaalka xaytiyo
Fad galbeed la moodaa
Kolkaad gelin is-dhugateen
Guluubkaagii shiikhoo
Dib-u guradku waa baqe?

Mise ganac-jabkaagiyo
Waxaad galabta mudataad
Intay goori goor tahay
Dayax soo lug-gu'i laa
Sii war-geli is-leedahay?

Gedgeddoonka hirarkee
Iyagoo garaaro leh
Gaatin-socodka laafyaha

The swing of her arms, the swing and the sway
Of her hips as she walks is just like the way
You sway and dip and the end of the day.
Now the clouds turn their backs on you.
They only have eyes for the eyes of the girl:
Eyes that launch love-darts, darts that sink
Into the flanks of the clouds and draw
Droplets of blood that stain the sky.
Setting sun
You're on the run:
Late afternoon
And gone so soon...
These are the lines
That seemed to fall
To hand when first
I saw the girl.
Now this is what
I most recall:
The way she reached up to gather fruit
Believing herself to be alone
Until she saw me there, wide-eyed,
As the wind read my mind and sent a gust
To part her dress and lay her breast
Bare for the space of an indrawn breath.
Ah, yes, I remember that...and the way
She caught at the cloth and fastened it,
Turning her face from mine, her eyes
Lowered, as if to say: No man
Has seen before what you saw today.

Xarragada u gaarka ah
Goonyahaaga tiiciyo
Gaardiga daruuraha
Kugu gaaf-wareegee
Gumucaad ridaysiyo
Goolli-baadh fallaadhaha
Shafka kaga garaacdee
Isu rogay guduudkee

Dhiiggooda gobo'liyo
Giirgiirka caadka leh
Ku sibbaaqday guudkiyo
Gara-saar-dabtoodii
Maxaa maanta gaasirey?
Miyay kugu giriifeen?

Mise waxay ka giigeen
Gobaad haybaddeediyo
Gantaalaha jacaylkiyo
Kalgacaylka beereey
Indhaheedu ganayaan?

Afartaa siddiri-gam
Waxaan gocanayaa weli

Tiiyoo gareyskiyo
Marta debec u gunuddoo
Guranaysa hoobaan
Oo aan geyaankeed
Geesaha ka filanayn
Dabayshii gadoodee
Uurkayga garatee
Gaadmada ku qaaddee
Gosha iyo horaadkiyo
Gaaddada u faydiyo
Garba-duubka maraday
Durba "geb" isku siisiyo
Gabbashada xishoodka ah
Gorodday lulaysiyo
Ugubnimo-gandoodkii.

SEER

Maxamed Xaashi Dhamac 'Gaarriye'

The literal translation of this poem was made by Martin Orwin. The
final translated version of the poem is by W N Herbert.

In my cradle I heard the women sing
'In the name of God, "Yaasin"':
this is how we begin,
with the dance step and the dance.
I was playing 'biito biiti',
singing 'Bille-jire'–
this is how Gaarriye grew.

I suckled on hearsay, drank in lore:
'A cloud in the east means rest your feet,
the rain will trek to us.'
Dear friend, dear Burhaan, I was taught
there are two types of poem:
that which tells you how things are
and that with another agenda –
the people know which is which.

When she brought me up, Biliso said,
'If a poem is a farm
then how things truly are, that's water;
the best words for the best thoughts,
that's how it begins.
Justice is your only compost,
life itself is what you hoe:
just squeeze truth from what happens
and in its own time it will sprout.

'Whether a poem brings forth seeds
depends on how it's tended and by whom –
the spot in which it's planted;

UURKUBBAALE

Maxamed Xaashi Dhamac 'Gaarriye'

'Cawdu billoo balooy baydh.'
'Bismillaahi "Yaasiin"'.
Botorkiyo ciyaartoo
Sidaa lagu bilaaboo,
Anna biito-biitiyo
Bille-jire ku dheelaan
Beri hore garaadsaday.

Dadka waxan ka bawsaday:
'Dhool bari ka hirey baa
Dhaanka loo bariiyaa'.
Gabaygana Burhaanoow
Waxa aniga lay baray
Inu laba u kala baxo
Beeshana u kala yahay:

Waxay Biliso igu tidhi:
'Hadday maanso beer tahay
Run baa lagu biyeeyaa.
Bilicsiga dareenkaa
Lagu baalaleeyaa;
Xaq baa lagu bac-rimiyaa.
Baaqbaaqa noloshiyo
Biyo-dhiijinteediyo
Xilligay ku biqishaa.

'Midho waxay u bixisaa
Habka loo barbaarshiyo
Barta lagu abqaalaa.
Sida loogu baahdaa

depending on who needs it and for what
its husk is hulled or boiled.

'A poem is the measure for
that trek beneath the draining sun
each generation adds to;
when you have to stand and fight
it shows you where to point the gun.

'It guides you like a conch shell horn,
the call of the large camel bell;
it is the words' own bugle.
It is the finest matting, woven for a bride,
the one the song calls 'Refuser of poor suitors'.
It's not sold for coppers,
it's not for praising the powerful;
to put a price on it, any price,
cheapens it and is forbidden.

'It's riding bareback on an unbroken horse –
you don't hobble its heels.
Those who fear for their hides
and won't ride without a saddle,
those lacking in the craft, can't get near this:
lies have nothing to do with it.
Poetry is a woman you do not betray,
to abuse her beauty is a sin.'

* * *

'It's most lovely when most perfectly timed,
as though, met at morning,
you exchanged greetings
at just the right moment.
When your own wings feel so bedraggled
that you need another's touch,
then the full beauty of a poem
is like a butterfly meeting
a just-wakened flower
at the exact moment of dawn.

Loo buushe-bixiyaa;
Ama loo bislaystaa.

'Waxa lagu bardaanshaa
Baqoolkiyo geeddiga
Fac kastaa intuu bogo.
Bullashada dagaalkana
Bunduqay tilmaantaa.

'Waa buun wax lagu hago;
Boodaanta yeedhmada
Bigil ereygu leeyahay.
Caws baar leh weeyaan;
Lana baxay sabool-diid
Soddon laguma baayaco.
Boqor laguma caabudo.
Biidhi-qaatennimiyo
Baqas waa ka xaaraan.

'Waana biime liidda ah,
Boqnihiisa lama xidho.
Nin baqdaa ma halabsado;
Bayd-gaabku kuma galo;
Beentana wax kuma laha.
Waa Bilan ma-geyno ah;
Bog-dooxeedu waa sino.'

           * * *

'Waxay bilic wax dheer tahay;
Iyadoon bariidada
Ballankeedi ka hor dhicin,
Kolkay bocorta maansado,
Adoo baalku kaa qoyey
Xadantana u baahnaa,
Sidii baalalleey iyo
Balanbaallis qalimo leh,
Ooy ubax baraarugay
Isku waa-bariisteen.

'When it seems to caress your flank,
to massage a salve into you;
when the pupil of its arrow pierces you
striking the mark exactly,
splitting your anguished cries in two.
Like a seer who peers inside you,
it homes in on your over-sensitivities,
your innermost wounds.

'When you suddenly hear of your betrothal
it sends the message deeper
into your most vulnerable point.
Poetry is the mine-seeker
opening your old, scarred-over hurt,
discovering your untouched earth,
that place closed off
from those closest to you.

'When Baahi-laawe, that dancing verse,
brushes the melancholy from you
as though it were a dust
that settled on your lust for life,
choked the desire in your chest;
it's like a grenade, a bomb,
its blast-range perfectly judged
so each stanza touches you
from problematic top to troubled toe,
exploding from your core.

'When it permeates you
each time a line is recited
as though from a secret page
on which your own secrets are exposed
so that each time you scan it
you jolt with anxiety.'

This poem alliterates in 'b'
but all the best poems are branded
so that each page which is turned

'Bogga kuu salaaxdee
Burcad kuugu duugtee,
Bu'da leebka kugu mudan
Baydari-abbaartee,
Bulxankeedu laba-dhaca
Sida uur-ku-baalaha,
Boogahaaga hoosiyo
Bayrtaada qoomee.

'Kolba baaq xiloodin ah
Barta aad u nogoshahay
Intuu baac u sii dego,
Tixda miino-baadhkii
Fiix kugu biskootiyo
Dhul bacdii ku taal iyo,
Ku banayso meel aan
Beryahaaba gacal dayin.

'Ee baahi-laawuhu
Adigoo basiiro leh
Intuu boodhka kaa tumo,
Xiisaha basaasiyo
Beer-qaado laabtee,
Tuduc wali gun iyo baar
Meel baas ku taabtee,
Intuu baaxad le'eg yahay
Isagoo banbaane ah
Badhtankaaga ka sanqadho.

'Ee kugu ballaadhee
Markii bayd la sheegaba,
Sidii baal qarsoodi ah
La bac dhabay xogtaadii,
Hadba baallo-daymada
Faraq-bood ka qaaddee.'
Maansada ba'leeyda ah
Ee baadi-soocda leh,
Bog kastoo la soo rogo
Sir aad bixisay mooddee,

makes you believe you've confessed
and each time your soul
involuntarily cries out, 'Bravo!
Dear God, don't seal this man's lips –
may the truth he speaks continue
as though it burst from my own mouth.'

Nafta oo baraad li'i:
Kolba 'baga!' tidhaahdiyo,
'Bishmaha Eebbe kuma jaro.
Ninka yidhi run badanaa!
Ma afkaygu kala baxay?'

SHE

Maxamed Xaashi Dhamac 'Gaarriye'

The literal translation of this poem was made by Martin Orwin
and Maxamed Xasan 'Alto'. The final translated version of the
poem is by David Harsent

Is she milk, is she more, is she buttermilk?
Is she bread, is she bread and milk, is she?
Would you say she's good luck? Would you say
She's a riddle, or maybe the answer?
Is she kindness or thought when it's solemn?
Is she thought, is she more - an idea?

Is she clouds that give rain, clouds that gather,
Clouds that bless, clouds that crowd, clouds that linger?
Would you say she's good luck, would you say
She's the pattern of stars struck at nightfall
When the day will bring cloudwrack and rainfall?

Would you say she's green growth in the rainfall?
Would you say she's the sun in the morning
That soaks up the dew, that disperses
The mist? Is she water that gathers
In pools after rain? Is she moonlight
Reflected in pools? Is she starlight
So bright when it floods with the moonlight
That you're blind to the land that you stand on?

Would you say she's green growth that the rainfall
Has washed and made sweet? Is she water
That lies on the land like a blessing?
Is she herself sweet, is she shapely?
Is her sweetness the perfume of water?

CARSHIGII JAMAALKA

Maxamed Xaashi Dhamac 'Gaarriye'

Ma cawaa ma caanaa
Ma ciirtaa ma calaf baa
Ma cuq baa ma cigashaa
Ma cisaa ma culuq baa
Ma daruur gu' curatoo
Cir caddaad an noqon baa
Ma cigaalka feleggiyo
Cirjiidkii mariiqaa
Ma magool cusayb baa
Ma cadceed arooryoo
Falaadhaha casuustaleh
Ku cabsiisay dheeggoo
Ceeryaantii didisaa
Ma xareed is celisaa
Ma habeen cadda ah oo
Balliyada cigaagani
Casuumeen xiddigahoo
Sida camal muraayad ah
Cirka dayaxi kaa jiray
Dhulka kaa cawaray baa
Cosob rayska xaadhiyo
Ma gargoorkii ceegoo
Calyayada barkaday baa.

Alla sama cuddoonaa
Udugaa carfoonaa
Samsam caynka loo dhigay

Is she beautiful, thoughtful and clever?
Does she live as she should? Does she honour
The qualities womanhood stands for?

You can see she's not weak and not foolish;
You can see she's not lazy and sluttish,
Not stubborn or sloppy or rowdy,
Neither a shrew nor a nag, she's
A woman who keeps a full larder,
A woman who'd greet you and feed you.

She's the lie of the stars that brings rainfall,
Not the set of the stars that brings drought to
The lie of the land that you stand on.

She's not fat, she's not thin, she is perfect.
She is modest - she dresses discreetly -
But it's clear that her body is perfect.

Oh, Cabdi, you see her as I do -
The way that she sways as she walks is
The reason I call her Catiya,
Catiya, whose walk is a rhythm
That chimes with my heart when I see her.

In the evening, she brushes her hair from
The crown to the tip and the breeze lifts
Each strand, so the eyes of the young men
Follow the stroke and the windblown
Hair as it catches the last of
The sun as it sets and makes firebrands,
Black but shot through with the sunset.

The colour of Catiya's skin is
The colour that all women envy.
Her eyes, soft and brown, are the eyes of
The desert gazelle, while her nose is
Perfectly straight and her gums are
Black, black as charcoal. Oh, Cabdi,
The white of her teeth and the down on
Her cheek! Can you see how her waistline

Citibaaro badanaa
Calle ma aha liiti ah
Habac maaha ceebaleh
Qallef maaha camal ba'an
Coon maaha loo hoyan
Baali maaha caaryaleh
Cirir maaha toomama
Cawro maaha socod badan
Cayil maaha laga dido
Caatana u may bixin
Cid kastaba u geeyoo
Meel laga canaantiyo
Cillad loo ma heli karo
Cabdiyow tallaabada
Cutiyaan idhaahdaa
Timahay caweyskii
Cirifyada u saartee
Ku cayaara leydhee
Haldhaayaduna cawryaan
Indhaheeda cawsha ah
Mus cideedka midabka ah
Sanqadhoodhka caynaba
Timaheeda culayga ah
Ciridkeeda dhuxusha ah
Ilkahaa caddaanka ah
Camankeeda xaaddaleh
Dhexda caara dhuubta ah
Cududaha garaaraha
Kubabkay u culustahay
Cambarshaha sudhkeeday
Firirsheen cabbaaryadu
Waa Xuur al-Caynoo
Kolba anigu tin iyo cidhib
Cad aan quudho kuma arag
Cagfudayd u may dhalan
Cadho lagu ma sheegeyn
Waa canaadi lama odhan

Is curved like a spear; can you see how
Her arms make an elegant shape in
The air as she moves, how her calves flex,
How her neck, with its dapple of amber,
Lightly creases: the neck of a Houri.

There is nothing to fault in this woman,
Not a flaw to be found in her beauty.
She is never impatient or angry;
She never complains. Could you weary
Of a woman like that? She could never
Lie or be troublesome. No one
Ever spoke ill of this women:
Her soft speech, her quick mind, her modest
Way in the world - this young woman
Whose future, I know, will be brighter
By far than the star of the evening.

Oh, Cabdi, you see her as I do:
A child who is almost a woman,
In the very first flush of her beauty.
I praise her. I crown her with garlands.
Haadrawi, match my song with your song.

Carrabkeedu beentiyo
Ma yaqaano caydaba
Wax ka cawda maan maqal
Ma cod dheera waa gabadh
Xishood baa u caado ah
Cimri waa u gaban weli
Caqli waa u waayeel
Cidhib baanay leedahay.

Aniguna ma caasiyo
Cadraddii ammaan lehe
Carshigii jamaalkaan
U caleemo saaraye
Adna cadar Hadraawow
Hambalyada u soo curi

DEATH OF A PRINCESS

Maxamed Xaashi Dhamac 'Gaarriye'

The literal translation of this poem was made by Martin Orwin
and Maxamed Xasan 'Alto'. The final translated version of the
poem is by W N Herbert

Xaye cala salaa
Come to prayer
Xaye cala falaax
Come to salvation
I can't remember
which prayer time it was
but I had to answer.
It may be the way of this world
beneath the witness of the stars
but last night I was told,
'They gorged on clotted blood.'

The earth there is dry and gleaming
scraped smooth
like camel fat.
All the goats and sheep
have grazed the land bare.

The place is ridden with ticks,
a desert where no-one can rest,
a scrubland sitting on oil;
floods of people with guns
and without restraints
surround it.

The place is duned,
with a humid wind;
it is, perhaps, the hottest time.

GEERIDII INA BOQOR

Maxamed Xaashi Dhamac 'Gaarriye'

'Xaye cala salaa'
'Xaye calal falaax'
Xilli loo addimay
Ma xusuusan karo;
Xilna waa jiraa
Waana xaal-adduun;
Xiddigihi cirkana
Xalaa laygu yidhi:
"Xinjireey liqeen".

Dhulku wuu xarkagay
Sidii xuuko geel
Waanu xiiran yahay.
Xooluhu dhammaan
Waa xaaluf-daaq.

Xaggu waa qaniin
Xaggu lama-degaan;
Xidhku waa saliid,
Daad-xoor dab-liyo
Xadhig-lama-sitaan
Ku dul xeeran yiin.

Xaggu waa bacaad
Xanfar iyo dabayl;
Malaa waa xagaa.

Xaggu waa masniyo
Fooq iyo xaraar

It is also cities
sprouting skyscrapers
which exhaust the eye,
furnished and fringed
with damask and silk;
they eavesdrop on air's gossip.
This is where those responsible
hoard their possessions.

Rivers flow within that land
waters of the Holy Places
and whisky foam
and froth up there.

The place is misery itself,
women burdened with children
hawking and gasping,
bearers and bricklayers
ground down and harassed.

My first quarter is done.
Look still more closely:
see our young woman, Xiis,
wholesome as a honeycomb,
born within the pale.
Like the choicest virgin mare,
she isn't bridled for
some camel raid, nor
a share of the loot.

She is Heaven's eye, a houri;
she is the sun, sharing
the horizon with the moon
who last night guarded the earth
and this morning passes on
his watch, elegantly
drawing back the hem,
the membrane of the sky
like closed curtains.

Isha xiijiyoo;
Demesh iyo xariir
Ku xiddaysanoo
Cirka soo xansada.
Oo dad loo xil-qabo
Xamastoodu taal.

Togag baa dhex xula;
Biyii Xaramka iyo
Wiski xooriyaa
Dhex xumbaynayaan.

Xaggu waa dar-xumo;
Xaawaleey carruur
Ku xansheeran oo,
Xiiq iyo harraad
Xuurteeysan iyo
Xammaal iyo wastaad.

Afartaasi xidhan.

Xaggan kalena eeg:
Gabadheenna Xiis
Waa xabag-barsheed;
Waa xero-u-dhalan
Xulad geenyo ugub.
Oon xiito guluf
Dirir iyo xabbaadh
Loo sudhin xakame.

Waa xuural-cayn;
Iyo Xaaliyeey
Dayax xoosh ahoo
Xalay gaadh ahaa,
Saakana xarrago
Xil-wareejintii,
Xuubkii cirkiyo
Daahyadi xidhnaa
Kor u xaydayoo;

He paints the dawn sky
as she rises in her urgency
with the fletches on the arrows
of the morning's rays.

And she, in this flirtation,
because of his caresses,
these delicate advances,
lets herself be roused.

In her fever and her heat,
her rising and ripping,
self-consuming passion,
she throws off her clouds
and stands, the length of a forearm
from the horizon. Can you see
her whip-lithe limbs?
If I've failed
then ask her to forgive me.

                                        * * *

Dearly-missed, our Xiis
was a navel to the river
of the people; she was part of them,
but penned in scrubland,
and fenced in the pen,
she did not have to see
that season which sears the trees,
feel its harshness or its heat.

Only once did she break out
only once feel the freedom
of transgressing their strictures.
It was said of Eve that she
cut the rope that bound her,
breached her limits.

And so she tore the silk off
that used to cover the hole

Sagal xaradhyo lihi
Qorrax xiiso wado,
Xaraaraha bulka leh
Ku xiddeeyeyoo;

Xod-xodtooy iyana
Xaradhaamadiyo
Hab-xiloodintii
Xadantootayoo;

Xummad iyo kulayl
Naf-xaraare baas,
Xaam-xaamadkii
Xayn furatay oo
Xusul joogga le'eg.
Xaashaa kallaa!
Xubno-jeedalleey
Haddii aan xistiyey
"Xaal qaado" dhaha.

                    * * *

Gabadheenna Xiis
Xubin bay ahayd
Xuddun webi ku taal;
Oo xidh oodan iyo
Xakab loo dugsiyo;
Oon xagaaga arag
Dhirta xaalufshiyo
Xanaf iyo kulayl.

Mar uun bay 'xaf' tidhi;
Mar uun bay Xorriyo
Ka kufriday xumii;
Laye Xaawo hee!
Xadhka-gooysayaa;
Xadki jabisayaa.

Is-xabaal wax badan
Godka uu xabkiyo

in which the rat eats
afterbirth and blood clots,
deliberately exposing
its shameful weaknesses,
its irresponsibilities:
she set them out one by one.

That tree, the twigs
and dry branches of which were kindling,
the dead leaves a fuel
which used to threaten fire,
she confirmed to the people
as hollow, a tree
of poisonous resin.

She disclosed our strongest feelings,
that intense intimacy of love,
which enters into us all;
she longed for her elegant boy
who swept her away;
by not closing off
her clean desires,
she refused stability.

She didn't consider how,
betrothed through obligation,
she was another man's wife;
nor took into account
that place she came from,
nor, poor girl,
the law that holds sway there.

                                    * * *

As this liaison continued
it went beyond whispers.
As soon as the secret was out
the family of that princess,
those wrong-doers,
grew wrathful;

Xinjiraha ku cuno,
Huwin jirey xariir
Ka xayuubisaa;
Xin u qaawisaa;
Ceebaha xilka leh
Xabbad-qaaddayaa.

Geedkii xaskiyo
Xuladada wax guba
Xaabuu u yahay
Loogu xeeban jirey,
Inu xabag-dhunkaal
Xordan yahay dadkii
U xaqiijisaa.

Xubbi iyo kalgacal
Laab xuunsho galay
La xariidisaa;
Dareenkeeda xalan
Iyadoon xidh-xidhin,
Hanadkii xasladay
Xiiseeysayaa;
Xasil diiddayaa.

Xusbaddana ma gelin
Inay xilo nin tahay
Qasab loogu xidhay;
Xaaleeyna-mayn
Xaafaddeey ka timi,
Iyo Xaaliyeey
Xeerkii ka jirey.

* * *

Waxay xawlisaba
Xanti durugtayaa;
Xogsigii horeba
Xigtadii Gobaad,
Dir-xumaan-ku-nool
Ka xanaaqdayaa;

that gluttonous House
got angry.

That gifted girl
was found guilty of what?
Love that was tethered to
'the branch with short roots
that can't reach the heights;
the wild choice
of the wrong ram' –
so they threw her in jail.

Then, although no-one tried her,
that Holy Place of love
which was a seat for
her clean heart,
that shrine to passion
was opened by a bullet.

This is how it was told:
she and the boy she loved
were cut down
and put in their graves.

If you only remember one thing
about this story, let it be this:
the place is Hijaz,
the centre of the divine revelation,
destination of the hajj;
it is the navel of the Prophet,
where the Beloved of God was born.

Baha-xaydho-weyn
Xayraantayaa.

Gabadhii Xaddiyo
Caashaqa ku xidhay
"Laan-gaabka xune
Xagga sare ahayn,
Xulashada gurracan
Ee sumal-xadka ah"
Ku xujoowdayaa;
Xabsi loo diryaa.

Iyadoon Xorriyo
Aan cidi xukumin
Qalbigii xallaa,
Xaramkii cishqiga
Xadradoow ahaa,
Taalladi xubbiga
Xabbad lagu furyaa.

Laye Xaadsan iyo
Xuurkeey jeclayd
Loogu xiiryeyaa;
La xabaalyeyaa.

Halna waa xusuus
Sheekada ku xidho:
Meeshu waa Xijaas
Xaruntii waxyiga
Halka loo xaj tago,
Ee Xabiibalaah
Xudduntiisu tahay.

HOOYO

Maxamed Ibraahim Warsame 'Hadraawi'

Translated as Mother by Martin Orwin

Oh mother without you
The world certainly
Would never have left night
Light not been found
People not have trekked
To a star over the Hawd
Would not have flown
Like birds of prey
To the moon in the clouds
Not have sent rockets
That appear like waves in the sky
Nor reached into space
Oh mother you've guided
The servants of God
To where they are today
With numbers I cannot
Calculate or count
The number of great people
You carried on your back
That you suckled
That you nourished
From your breast

When you bear a man
With support of his kin
Whose camels men fear to raid

The Hawd is a major grazing area in eastern Ethiopia inhabited by Somalis.

HOOYO

Maxamed Ibraahim Warsame 'Hadraawi'

Hooyoy la'aantaa
Adduunyadu hubaashii
Habeen kama baxdeenoo
Iftiin lama heleenoo
Dadku uma hayaameen
Xiddig hawd ka lulatoo
Sida haad ma fuuleen
Dayax heego joogoo
Hubka laguma tuureen
Hawo laguma gaadheen
Cirka hirar ka muuqdoo
Hooyoy addoomuhu
Halkay maanta joogaan
Adigow horseedoo
Intaad hanad xambaartee
Haaneedka siisee
Horaaddada jaqsiisee
Habtay baan xisaab iyo
Tiro lagu heleynoo.

Marka aad nin hiilloo
Laga baqo hashiisiyo
Halyey diran dhashaabaa
Hooyo lagu xusuustaa

Marka aad nin hoo-loo
Gurigiisa habaqluhu
Isku soo halleeyoo
Hayntiisa quudhoo

A steadfast hero
Mother, you are remembered for it.

When you bear a generous man
Who says 'Please, take this.'
Who when a visitor
Arrives with nothing
Gives of his wealth
Coming closer to God
A man people wish
Would never die
Mother, you are remembered for it.

When you bear a man
Who in his intention
Follows a straight path
When he meets one wave
Then deals with the next
Who guides his dependents
Whom all wish to emulate
Mother, you are remembered for it.

When you bear a man who stands
Against disaster and war
Who understands the true law
Deliberates on the truth
Dampens conflict and danger
When it's set alight
Who prevents bloodshed
Gives order to the people
Leads them all
Mother, you are remembered for it.

When you bear a famous poet
Who knows the construction and decoration
The composition and the tuneful chant
Tightly forming the words of poetry
Which God has given as a gift
The artist who shapes all this
Mother, you are remembered for it.

Hor Ilaahay geystiyo
Lama hure dhashaabaa
Hooyo lagu xusuustaa.

Marka aad nin himilada
Hilin toosan mariyoo
Hir markii la gaadhoba
Ku labaad hilaadshoo
Haga maatadiisoo
La higsado dhashaa baa
Hooyo lagu xusuustaa.

Marka aad nin hooggiyo
Ka hor taga dagaalkoo
Garta hubin yaqaanoo
Xaqa hoos u eegoo
Halistiyo colaadaha
Dabka hura bakhtiiyoo
Ku haggoogta dhiiggoo
Dadka kala hagaajoo
Kala haga dhashaa baa
Hooyo lagu xasuustaa.

Markaad hoobal caaniyo
Hindisaa farshaxanoo
Hab-dhaca iyo luuqdiyo
Hawraarta maansada
Heensayn yaqaannoo
Rabbi hibo u siiyo
Labadaba hannaanshiyo
Hal-abuur dhashaa baa
Hooyo lagu xasuustaa.

Dumar iyo haween baa
Nolol lagu haweystaa
Kuwa lagu hammiyayee
Sida hawd caleen weyn
Rag u wada hamuumee
Ishu halacsanaysaa
Hablahaaga weeyee

Women are desired in life
The ones sought after
Like a forest of fresh leaves
Men are hungry, and what
They set their eyes on
Are those young women of yours
When marriage is discussed
It is a girl, a tall heego cloud
Like ripe fruit, rich
In strength, maturity and beauty,
It's Hira, that one marries
Mother, you are remembered for it.

Oh mother without you
Language would not be learnt
Oh mother without you
Speech would be impossible
There is no one in the world
You did not bring up
To whom you haven't sung,
Haven't calmed with lullabies,
Not one who lacked you efforts
In reaching maturity
That compassion has not covered
In the house of love.

Oh mother through you
Peace is made certain
Oh mother on your lap
The child falls to sleep
Oh mother, by your hem
Shelter is found
Oh mother, the infants
Benefit from your teaching
You gladden the camel calf
You, the rain cloud that cools
You, the essential sleeping mat
You, the clean shelter
You, a heritage all journey towards.

Marka guur la haybshee
Gabadh heego dheeroo
Hoobaan la moodoo
Karti iyo hub-qaadloo
Quruxdana ka hodaniyo
Hira[1] laga aroostaa
Hooyo lagu xusuustaa.

Hooyoy la'aantaa
Higgaad lama barteenoo
Hooyoy la'aantaa
Hadal lama kareenoo
Ruuxaanad habinoo
Kolba aanad hees iyo
Hoobey ku sabinoo
Hawshaada waayaa
Hanaqaadi maayee
Hoygii kalgacalkee
Naxariistu hadataay.

Hooyoy dushaadaa
Nabad lagu hubaayoo
Hooyoy dhabtaadaa
Hurdo lagu gam'aayoo
Hooyoy taftaadaa
Dugsi laga helaayoo
Waxa lagu hal-maalaa
Hooyo ababintaadee
Hayin lagu badhaadhaay
Hogol lagu qaboobaay
Gogol lama huraaneey
Dugsigii hufnaantaay
Hidda lagu arooraay.

---

[1]This is the name of a woman representing a woman of good virtue and beauty.

Mother while you live
I anoint you with congratulations
Greetings and wealth
I cover you with respect and esteem
Mother, your death
Is my disaster
In both body and mind
I hold your memory
I sing still for you
Above your grave
I wear the mourning cloth
Knowing that better than here
Where the birds fly
The animals roam
Where all creation lives
By the gift of God
Better than all this
Is the hereafter.

Intaad hooyo nooshahay
Hambalyiyo salaan baan
Hanti kaaga dhigayaa
Hamrashiyo xaq-dhowr baan
Dusha kaa huwinayaa,
Hooyo dhimashadaaduna
Hooggayga weeyoo
Hiyiga iyo laabtaan
Kugu haynayaayoo
Weligey hoggaagaan
Ka dul heesayaayoo
Hengel baan u xidhiyaa
Inta haadka duushiyo
Idil habar dugaaggee
Ifka hibo ku noolow
Aakhiro halkii roon.

PROFILE OF TRANSLATED POETS

Axmed Shiikh Jaamac, was born in Las Anood District in 1942 and completed a degree in Journalism at the National University in Mogadishu. Ahmed was an Arabic teacher at the Ministry of Education of the former Republic of Somalia. Following the collapse of Siad Barre's regime he moved to Yemen and worked for Al-Miithaaq, a Yemeni journal in which he published a weekly column. He since returned to Somalia and is now a director of the Puntland Ministry of Information, Telecommunications, Culture and Heritage in Garowe.

Saado Cabdi Amarre is an amiable poet whose emotional verse laments the senselessness of the successive civil wars that have affected Somaliland in the aftermath of its secession. Her masterpiece 'Haddaba Deeqaay, dagaalkani muxuu ahaa' (roughly translated as 'O! Deeqa! What is the meaning of this war?') touched the hearts of many when it was first recited publicly in 1994 and her public readings have continued to attract enthusiastic audiences. A renowned dissident during Siad Barre's governance, she was a valued member of the Somali National Movement (SNM). She countinues to campain for peace through her thought-provoking writing and poignant delivery. She also serves her community working as a police officer.

Jaamac Kadiye Cilmi is a traditional poet whose work addresses a range of social and political issues. He is renowned for the creation of the 'Saar' rhythmic poetry form. Born in Las-Anod, Jama became a prominent poet throughout the Somali region and one of the few poets who compose and perform this form of art. He was part of 'Danaan', a military performance group. He currently lives in Goray, working with different community organisations to promote poetry.

Caasha Luul Mohamad Yusuf is quickly emerging as one of the most exciting young poets living in the Somali diaspora. Like all Somalis, Caasha grew up in a culture steeped in poetry and while she was young she started to compose her own poems. Her work began getting published on Somali websites in 2008 and, since then, she's rapidly garnered a great deal of praise for her ability to infuse her poetry with fresh imagery enlivened by telling details. Caasha came to the UK in 1990 having fled the Somali Civil War. She now has three children and a steady job and a growing career as a poet.

Maxamed Xaashi Dhamac 'Gaarriye' since the 1970s has been universally regarded as one of the most important Somali poets composing on a great variety of topics from nuclear weapons to Nelson Mandela. A poet who has never been afraid to engage in the politics of Somalia through his poetry, he was the initiator of one of the largest 'chain poems' 'Deelley' to which many poets contributed, each one alliterating in 'd' - hence the name of the chain.

Mahamed Ibrahim Warsame 'Hadraawi' is one of the greatest, most cherished and respected Somali poets and philosophers. Rightly hailed as a genius, he is a consciensious popular figure who fearlesslessly speaks for the defencless. His earlier work focused on love, producing poems like "Todobaadan Midhabley" and songs such as, "Baladweyn", "Jacayl Dhiig Malagu Qoray?", "Hooyooy", "Cajabey, Cajiibey". The songs of this era have been sung by some of the greatest Somali singers. In the 1970s, Hadraawi's artistic productions evolved to address more social and political themes. During this time Hadraawi co-wrote the landmark political play "Aqoon iyo Afgarad" with Gaarriye, Siciid Saalax and Musse Abdi Elmi. He also became occupied with the Siinlay chained poems, which attracted over twenty other poets to take part. All of this and two other plays put Hadraawi at odds with the Barre regime; he was put in jail for five years (from 1973 to 1978). Since his release, he has released numerous critically acclaimed poems and continues to show solidarity to those in need.

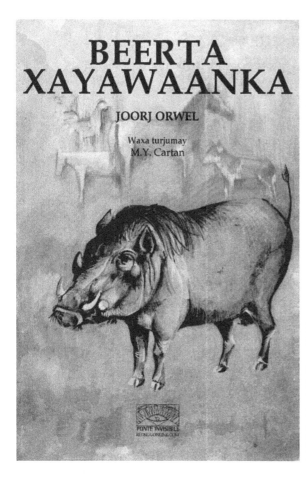

BEERTA XAYAWAANKA

JOORJ ORWEL

Waxa turjumay
M.Y. Cartan

PONTE INVISIBILE
REDSEA-ONLINE.COM

Iswaydaarsi
(Exchange) series No. 1

George Orwell
translated by Maxamed
Yuusuf Cartan
Beerta Xayawaanka
(Animal Farm),
ISBN 9788888934204
Pages 138, Pisa. 2011

George Orwell's "Animal Farm" translated by the late Mohamed Yuusuf Cartan is just published again with copyright permission. The book was one of the literature works that was distributed to the young readers in Somaliland to read in public excerpts during the Moving Library tour which was part of Hargeysa International Book Fair 2011.

The translation of this volume begins a new series of books called "Iswaydaarsi" (exchange) which intends to provide specific knowledge of the international classical literature to the young Somali speaking readership. The Iswaydaarsi series will also include renowned Somali literature translated into foreign language, with the ultimate objective being to harmonize the cultural exchange between written and oral traditions.

ANTON CHEKHOV

Sheekooyin la soo xulay
(Selected short stories)

Waxaa turjumay (Translated by)
Siciid Jaamac Xuseen

oo ay kaalmeeyeen (with the help of)
Rashiid Sheekh Cabdillaahi "Gadhwayne"
iyo Maxamed Xasan Cali "Alto"

PONTE INVISIBILE
WWW.REDSEA-ONLINE.COM

Iswaydaarsi
(Exchange) series No. 3

Anton Chekhov - sheekooyin la soo xulay
Waxa turjumay Siciid Jaamac Xuseen
Ponte Invisibile
Pisa, 2011
ISBN: 9788888934280
Price: 12.80 Euros

From the introduction: the essence of this attempt at translating some of Chekhov's short stories has been the fulfilment of the ambitious aim, albeit to a very small degree, of introducing the Somali reader to the cultural world of Chekhov through the glimpses of the realities Anton Chekhov artfully depicts in his own unique style of the world and culture of his time in Russia. Admittedly, no matter how hard we tried, we are non the less well aware of

JAAMAC MUUSE JAAMAC

Gobannimo bilaash maaha

Hiilka Qodobka 32

Gobannimo Bilaash Maaha!

Gogoldhigga
Cabdiraxmaan Maxamed Cabdillaahi "Cirro"

Qodobka 37ªª, ¹ⁱ²ʰ, ruhinta ¹ᵈ
Eebbaha wanaadda Somaliland ku hvenay geyganı axxa uu ugu deeqay axeed ıyo karaamo Qaranmimo. Sharciga Jamhuunyadda Somaliland axxa uu aaveddaas ıyo karaamadaas sidii ku cad Dastuurka u igmaday daa-lad ku dhivasaan doonta kuna dhapru doonta Dastuurka

Curisyo (Essays) Series No. 1
Gobannimo bilaash maaha
Jama Musse Jama
Ponte invisibile, Pisa, 2007, ISBN: 88-88934-06-5

The idea behind this publication was to explain to ordinary citizens the significance of Article 32 of the Somaliland constitution, which "guarantees the fundamental right of freedom of expression and makes unlawful all acts to subjugate the press and the media". The book, became part of a wider campaign in conjunction with Somaliland human rights groups for freedom of expression. Gobannimo Bilaash Maaha (roughly translated as 'freedom is not free'), was awarded by the Somaliland Writers' Association. In his book, the author has successfully themed the different levels of freedom, nationality, society, civil liberties and most importantly

Curisyo (Essays) Series No. 2
Ahmed Ibrahim Awale
Qaylo-dhaan deegaan / Environment in crises
Ponte Invisibile, Pisa, 2010, ISBN: 88-88934-13-8
21.00 Euro

Ahmed I. Awale's new book is the first of its type to deal with the highly important issue of environmental disasters, particularly looking at the impact of resource depletion on those whose livelihoods depend on these resources for their survival. Combining academic research with reflections from traditional knowledge, personal philosophies and faith, this book is accessible to a wide range of readers with an interest in Somali culture, the flora and fauna of the Somali regions, and the environmental challenges facing the people who live there. Bilingual in Somali and English, the book is a master piece of work, and is the second book of the Curisyo series.

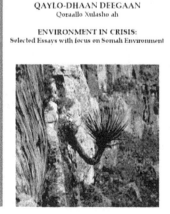

AHMED IBRAHIM AWALE

QAYLO-DHAAN DEEGAAN
Qoraallo Xulasho ah

ENVIRONMENT IN CRISIS:
Selected Essays with focus on Somali Environment

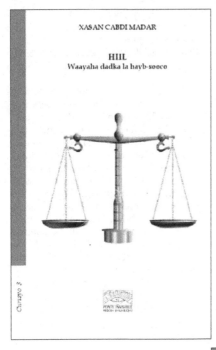

Curisyo (Essays) Series No. 3
HIIL by Xasan Cabdi Madar
Ponte Invisibile, Pisa, 2010
Price 12,80 Euro

Hassan Abdi Madar's book Hiil (In Defence of/'Hayb-sooco') tackles one of the major issues facing contemporary Somali society in the form of minority rights. It addresses the marginalisation and social exclusion of the 'Gabooye' communities.

Curisyo (Essays) Series No. 4
Adduun iyo taladii
Rashiid Sheekh Cabdillaahi Xaaji Axmed
Ponte Invisibile, Pisa, 2010, ISBN: 9966-7059-16-2
160 pages. Soft cover, 12,80.Euro

Adduun Iyo Taladii is a new book written by Rashid Sheikh Abdillahi 'Gadhwayne' which touches the essence of citizenship. 'Gadhweyne' is a scholar, social scientist, and literary critic. No other book is more at home in the Curis Series than the work of Rashid Sheikh Abdillahi 'Gadhwayne'. In his collection of essays Rashid deals with different aspects of citizenship, which are interconnected and fully complement each other. This book enlightens the reader on various subjects with vital impacts on the building blocks of each society by exploring the themes such as freedom, tolerance, righteousness, equality, and their true normative, ethical, deep moral meaning in the Somali context. It is a work which is inspired by his great sense of social responsibility.

Curisyo (Essays) Series No. 5
Shufbeel - tiraab soomaaliyeed
Siciid Jaamac Xuseen
ISBN 88-88934-22-8 EAN 9788888934228
Pages 126, Pisa, 2011

'Shufbeel' is a collection of essays and short stories, including modern and traditional Somali wisdom and entertainment (murti iyo madaddaalo). The author, Saed Jama is one of pilasters for the literary promotion in the Somali speaking society. Shuhbeel is the 5th and latest book of the Curisyo series collection. 'Curisyo' is a series of books, covering a ranging set of topics, yet share the spirit of citizenship. The series so far dealt with several themes, including Freedom of expression, Environment, Tolerence, Ethics, and more.

Curisyo series:

"Curisyo" is series of books published and distributed by Ponte Invisibile (redsea-online.com) and directed by Jama Musse Jama. "Curisyo" series of books contain essays which cover a ranging set of topics, yet share the spirit of citizenship.

Printed in the United States
By Bookmasters